Now We See the Church

Now We See the Church

Messages on the Life of the Church, the Body of Christ

Stephen Kaung

CHRISTIAN FELLOWSHIP PUBLISHERS, INC.
NEW YORK

Copyright © 2015
Christian Fellowship Publishers, Inc.
New York
All Rights Reserved.

ISBN: 978-1-68062-653-7

Available from the Publishers at:

11515 Allecingie Parkway
Richmond, Virginia 23235
www.c-f-p.com

Printed in the United States of America

Preface

This series of messages, delivered by the author before a Christian audience in Richmond, Virginia over a period of three years commencing in January 1996, serves as a follow-up companion volume to his series of messages on the life of the Lord Jesus Christ, which he had delivered before the same audience.[*] Having come to see Christ Jesus therein, we are now ready to see His church, about which Jesus had declared this: "I will build my [church], and hades' gates shall not prevail against it" (Matthew 16:18b). From this declaration we realize that the church is not the product of the work of man, but it is the Lord Jesus himself who builds the church. Hence, in Scripture, the church is called "the Christ" (I Corinthians 12:12c; Ephesians 3:4b, 8b Darby).

The New Testament book of Acts gives us a panoramic view of the churches in the first century. It also provides us with a prophetic picture of the churches throughout the centuries. As we review the histories of these various churches that are narrated for us in Acts, may we learn all the lessons God wants us to learn from them.

---

[*] See Stephen Kaung, *"But We See Jesus"; Messages on the Life of the Lord Jesus Christ* (New York: Christian Fellowship Publishers, 2015).

Contents

PREFACE	5
INTRODUCTION: THE BODY OF CHRIST	9
1. THE MYSTERY OF CHRIST	13
2. THE BIRTH OF THE CHURCH	27
3. THE CHURCH IN JERUSALEM	41
4. THE CHURCH IN ANTIOCH	63
5. THE CHURCHES IN GALATIA	81
6. THE CHURCH IN PHILIPPI	103
7. THE CHURCH IN THESSALONICA	125
8. THE CHURCH IN CORINTH	145
9. THE CHURCH IN EPHESUS	165
10. THE CHURCH IN COLOSSAE	183
11. THE CHURCH IN ROME	203
CONCLUSION: LESSONS TO BE LEARNED	219

Unless otherwise indicated,
Scripture quotations are from the
New Translation by J. N. Darby.

Introduction

THE BODY OF CHRIST

> Acts 1:1-5—*I composed the first discourse, O Theophilus, concerning all things which Jesus began both to do and to teach, until that day in which, having by the Holy Spirit charged the apostles whom he had chosen, he was taken up; to whom also he presented himself living, after he had suffered, with many proofs; being seen by them during forty days, and speaking of the things which concern the kingdom of God; and, being assembled with them, commanded them not to depart from Jerusalem, but to await the promise of the Father, which said he ye have heard of me. For John indeed baptised with water, but ye shall be baptised with the Holy Spirit after now not many days.*

I would like for us to meditate together on the life of the church, the body of Christ. At the beginning of the book of Acts the beloved physician Luke wrote: "I composed the first discourse, O Theophilus [meaning, Lover of God], concerning all things which Jesus began both to do and to teach, until that day in which, having by the Holy Spirit charged the apostles whom he had chosen, he was taken up."

The Gospel according to Luke, which was his first discourse, is composed of all things which Jesus began both to do and to teach. Thus, in his Gospel, Luke related all which Jesus had done and taught from the time of His incarnation up to the time He ascended to heaven. That was the context of Luke's first discourse.

Luke then composed a second discourse, and it is this book of Acts that in the original lacked the title *The Acts of the Apostles* but was simply entitled *The Acts*. Yet exactly whose acts are recorded in this second Lukan discourse? If the first one was concerned with what Jesus had *begun* both to do and to teach, then it should naturally follow that the second discourse is concerned with what He *continued* to do and to teach. When Jesus began to do and to teach, He did so in that incarnated body He had received from His mother Mary. But as one reads Luke's second discourse it needs to be asked: In what body did Jesus continue to do and to teach? Is it not quite evident that it was in the church, the body of Christ?

The Lord Jesus rose from the dead, ascended to heaven, and sent the Holy Spirit to the earth; by His finished work on the cross and the coming of the Holy Spirit, a new body for Him was formed. It is a mystical, corporate body. It is the body of Christ, even the church; and it is in this corporate body that the Lord Jesus continued back then to do and to teach and continues to do so even today. He is not only the foundation of the church, He is also the very life of the church.

I Corinthians 12:12 informs us: "even as the body is one and has many members, but all the members of the body, being many, are one body, so also is the Christ." Of course, we know this verse is describing the church because the church is one body with many members. Though we each physically are composed of many members, yet we each have but one body; and so also is the church, the body of Christ. Indeed, it is in one Spirit that we all, whether Jews or Gentiles, have been baptized into one body, and we all have been made to drink of that one Spirit (I Corinthians 12:13).

But strangely enough, we find in the I Corinthians 12:12 passage that the Holy Spirit, instead of moving Paul to employ the words "so also is the church, the body of Christ," He has the apostle write, "so also is the Christ." This is because the church is *the* Christ, the extension of Christ, the corporate expression

Introduction: The Body of Christ

of Christ. It is Christ himself in a corporate body, and it is in that body that the risen and ascended Jesus continues to do and to teach by the power of the Holy Spirit. During the period of time between the moment of His ascension and the moment of His anticipated return again to the earth, Jesus has been doing, working and teaching—yet not in that incarnated body but in the corporate, mystical body, which is the church. For this reason, we cannot have fully considered the life of Jesus Christ on the earth without also pondering the life of the church because it completes that earthly life of His.

Chapter One

THE MYSTERY OF CHRIST

Ephesians 3:1-11—For this reason I Paul, prisoner of the Christ Jesus for you nations, (if indeed ye have heard of the administration of the grace of God which has been given to me towards you, that by revelation the mystery has been made known to me, (according as I have written before briefly, by which, in reading it, ye can understand my intelligence in the mystery of the Christ,) which in other generations has not been made known to the sons of men, as it has now been revealed to his holy apostles and prophets in the power of the Spirit, that they who are of the nations should be joint heirs, and a joint body, and joint partakers of his promise in Christ Jesus by the glad tidings; of which I am become minister according to the gift of the grace of God given to me, according to the working of his power. To me, less than the least of all saints, has this grace been given, to announce among the nations the glad tidings of the unsearchable riches of the Christ, and to enlighten all with the knowledge of what is the administration of the mystery hidden throughout the ages in God, who has created all things, in order that now to the principalities and authorities in the heavenlies might be made known through the [church] the all-various wisdom of God, according to the purpose of the ages, which he purposed in Christ Jesus our Lord.

The life of the church, the body of Christ, began on the day of Pentecost because that is when the church was born; but that does not mean the concept of the church had its beginning at that time. To the contrary, if we carefully read the word of God, we learn that though the church was born on the day of Pentecost, the concept of the church was conceived in the heart of God well before the foundation of the world. Such is likewise true when speaking of the life of the Lord Jesus.

The Concept of Christ from Eternity Past

For we may recall that when previously we had considered together the life of the Lord Jesus[*], we had quite naturally begun with His incarnation because that was the moment of His birth, the beginning of the earthly life of Jesus. But as a matter of fact the concept of Jesus Christ had its beginning well before the foundation of the world. Even before God created all things He had conceived in His mind and in His very heart the concept of Christ. It is therefore not a human invention: no one could have invented a Christ, for as is recorded in God's word, that is something which eyes have not seen, ears have not heard, and has never come into anyone's mind (I Corinthians 2:9). We can therefore rightly say that the concept of Christ is a divine one.

Christ has His origin in God, not in the thought of man. Even before the creation of the world, God's eternal purpose concerning His beloved Son was to make Him heir of all things (Hebrews 1:2b). And with that purpose God created all things in His Son, by His Son, and for His Son (Colossians 1:16-17). Unfortunately, because of rebellion and sin—perpetrated by both the celestial and terrestrial beings whom He had created—all things began to disintegrate, to descend into chaos, and to become purposeless. God, of course, in His foreknowledge in eternity past, knowing that such a development would happen,

---

[*] See again Stephen Kaung, *"But We See Jesus"; Messages on the Life of the Lord Jesus Christ* (New York: Christian Fellowship Publishers, 2015).

conceived the idea of Christ—the Sent or the Anointed One—in accordance with that purpose which He had purposed for His Son. God would come with a mission in the person of Christ to recover and to reconcile all things back to His fullness. We are told in Ephesians that at the fullness of time God would sum up or gather up all things in Christ—both things in the heavens and things upon this earth (Ephesians 1:10). So the concept of Christ is from eternity past even though the life of Christ began at His incarnation.

There is one remarkable fact which should truly draw out worship from us; which is, that in reading the life of Christ as recorded in the four New Testament Gospels we discover that that earthly life was in perfect agreement—in perfect harmony, possessed of one hundred percent oneness—with the concept of Christ that God had conceived of in His thought. That earthly life of Jesus Christ was in accordance in every way with the divine concept, and the divine concept was fully fulfilled in that one earthly life. *That* is the glory of Christ, and that is something which should surely bring us into worship.

The Concept of the Church from Eternity Past

Now just as was the case with the origin of the concept of Christ, so it was with that of the church. We say that the life of the church began on the day of Pentecost in Jerusalem, but the concept of the church was conceived in the mind of God well before the world's foundation. In Ephesians 3 it is called "the mystery of the Christ"; and it was purposed in God through His Son long before the ages of time began. And by this church God is to manifest and make known His manifold wisdom to the principalities and authorities both in this age and in the ages to come (v.10).

God's concept—and therefore His decision and will—is to give His beloved Son an everlasting life companion—His like, His counterpart—and for that companion to be His body so as to contain all His Son's riches and to manifest His Son's glory; and further, to have that body so matured and perfected that it can be joined to His Son as His bride for eternity. God wants to have a people who are in total oneness with His beloved Son; that is to say, a people who, having His life, are being joined together with His Son in sharing in His sufferings, sharing in His glory, following Him in that age-long battle against the Enemy, and in assisting His Son in bringing all things back to God himself. That is the glorious concept of the church, the body of Christ. It is to be made up of many members, and yet it is only one body, the fullness of Christ who fills all and in all (Ephesians 1:22b-23). Such is the wonderful divine concept of the church, the body of Christ.

So the critical question today is: How close or how one is the life of the church with the divine concept of the church? The success or failure of the church is not to be measured by outward appearance—that is, by what one sees or hears. Rather, the success or the failure of the church is to be measured by its closeness to or its distance from the divine concept of the church. Why so? It is because the church is not a human invention; nor is it only an historical event; on the contrary, the church has its origin in God, having been conceived in the heart and mind of God. Therefore, unless the life of the church on earth agrees with the divine concept of the church in heaven, we have to say it is a failure; no matter how it appears to man, it is a failure. Only when the life of the church is one with the divine concept of the church can it be said that God's purpose is achieved.

For this reason, it is extremely important that we have a vision of what the church is. And by vision I simply mean: What is the church in the thought of God? What has He planned for the church? What is it that he is really after in His church? Unless we have this vision it is very difficult for us to truly enter into the life of the church in the way which will please God. So it needs to be emphasized that we need to ask God to give us revelation as to what the church is in His mind, so that by His grace we may be one in our church life with the divine concept of the church. That concept or vision determines what the life of the church will be; and hence, it is *that* important.

The Church Hidden in the Old Testament

As noted earlier, the church had been conceived in the mind of God before the foundation of the world. It was so sacred a matter that God hid it in himself for the longest time. It was called a "mystery" in God's word. A mystery is not something mysterious; it simply means it is a secret that needs to be uncovered and revealed. We may say that the church had been a top-secret matter to God. It was so sacred a thing that it took a very long time for Him to reveal it to man because it was beyond man's comprehension. Unless God would reveal it we would never know it; and furthermore, as flawed human beings our moral and spiritual condition has been such that God was not able to reveal the concept of the church all at once. It required a long, long time and a long period of preparation before God was able to fully reveal to us what the church is. In short, it remained for the longest time a closely-held top secret with God. Nevertheless, we thank God that through the ages He was moved to drop hints here and there. They merely served as clues along the way; even so, we can discern how God had desired to reveal to us that top secret of His because it was so dear to Him.

The Mystery Hinted at through the Creation of Man

Let us take note, for instance, of one of the first hints, that which is in regard to the creation of man. In the Old Testament book of Genesis we read that God said, Let us make man in our image, after our likeness. And in His image, according to His likeness, He made man; male and female he created them (Genesis 1:26-27). This latter statement is very strange, in that according to God's image He made the man in His likeness; and yet, immediately following these words the Scripture declares that God created them male and female. In other words, the man whom God created is two in one: him and them—the them being male and female. Let us recall that in the process of creating, God took up red earth and formed the body of a man (Genesis 2). Then God breathed into his nostrils the breath of life and man became a living soul—that was Adam, the male (v.7). Later on, He put Adam to sleep, opened up his side, and took out *something*. Our English-language Bibles read: a rib; but the original Hebrew word is to be more accurately translated as *something*. Now with that something which He took out of man God built a woman: *ishshah*—meaning "woman out of man." Therefore, when Adam woke up and God led the woman to Adam, the man looked at Eve and said, "Now this is I myself, bone of my bone and flesh of my flesh." And they were united into one flesh (vv.18-24).

We know that this fact of the beginning of mankind is a type of that eternal reality of Christ and His church. Christ came into this world to find a bride, but He could find her nowhere; and because of this, God put Him to death. With Adam it was just a sleep, but with the Lord Jesus it was death because sin had entered this world. With Adam it was a bloodless surgery and totally painless, but with the Lord Jesus it was a bloody death and extremely painful because sin had entered this world. And as was the case with Adam we learn from Scripture that God likewise opened up Jesus' side by a soldier having thrust a spear into His side (John 19:34)—it reaching deeply inward into His very heart—and out of His side came forth blood and water. That was the *something* out of Him: blood and water.

We may further recall from John 19 that the apostle John wrote copiously with regard to this moment of Jesus' side being pierced: "I saw it; I bear witness to it; and this witness which I bear is true so that you may believe" (v.35). Why did he stress so much this particular detail surrounding Jesus' crucifixion? The apostle has explained it in another of his New Testament writings; for John wrote in I John 5:6 that "he [Jesus] ... came by water and blood." In other words, it is Jesus' blood that has been shed for the remission of our sins. His precious outpoured blood washes our sins away. Water, on the other hand, betokens His life poured forth that we may receive life eternal. And these become the material for the building of the church—the *ishshah*, the woman out of man. It is because the church comes out of Christ and is built with the very life of Christ that therefore the church can be His like, His counterpart. The church can be joined together with Him in one Spirit. And so, it is by this analogy that God has given us a further hint of the mystery of Christ and the church so that we may understand.

The Mystery Hinted at through the Nation of Israel

Throughout the Old Testament we can pick up hints here and there, but let us use the illustration of the children of Israel as a further hint. We know that the history of the children of Israel began with Abraham, whom God called. The God of glory appeared to Abraham and He called him out of his native land and separated him; and because of his obedience and his faith in God, He made a covenant with him. God promised Abraham that a seed—a nation—would come out of him, and that even the whole world would be blessed by that seed. It is because of Abraham that God chose the children of Israel. They were not chosen because of their righteousness; on the contrary, they were a stiff-necked, highly rebellious people, and God told them so. They were only chosen because of their father, Abraham. God then delivered them out of Egypt and brought them into the Promised Land of Canaan, yet not because they were many in number: as a matter of fact, they were actually the fewest in number (Deuteronomy 7:6-7); no, God did it because He kept His promise—His covenantal promise to Abraham, to Isaac, and to Jacob. He set the Israelites apart to make them His peculiar possession. God committed and entrusted His name to them, and tested them for forty years in the wilderness to prove what was in their heart. Unfortunately, they were unfaithful to God.

In I Corinthians 10 we are told that all these things concerning the Israelites were recorded for our admonition. They were included in the Old Testament narrative as types and shadows. They were recorded there in order to instruct us who live at the end of time (vv.1-12, especially vv.6, 11). Do we not see that there is a similarity there between God's chosen people in the Old Testament era and us today? We are chosen not because of what we are, for like the Israelites we were a rebellious, stiff-necked people. No, we are chosen because of Christ. It is not because of our righteousness that God has delivered us out of the power of darkness and translated us into the kingdom of the Son of His love. It is because God is faithful. Out of His love He uses the history of the children of Israel to instruct us and to warn us in order that we would not follow the same path as they did. We should learn lessons from that.

The Church Partially Revealed in the Gospels

When Jesus came to this earth, we know that deep in His heart He came for one purpose—to seek for His body, His bride—the church. Oddly enough, however, in the record of His life which we have in the four Gospels, that word church is mentioned only twice. Throughout His adult years on earth Jesus mentioned the church only twice; yet that was what was in His heart. Even so, He kept the matter within His heart because it was not yet time to reveal it. The church could not be revealed fully until He had accomplished the work of redemption.

"I Will Build My Church"

Only when Peter confessed Him as the Christ, the Son of the living God (a revelation given to him by the Father, be it noticed), could Jesus no longer keep that secret from His chosen disciples. So He said, "I say to you, you are Peter, a little stone, and on this rock I will build My church; and the gates of Hades shall not prevail against it" (see Matthew 16:17-18).

While Jesus was on earth He did not build a church. Instead, He was gathering materials for it, His work being similar to what King David had done. David's desire had been to build God a house—the temple at Jerusalem, and God was pleased with that desire. Nevertheless, David did not build the temple during his lifetime; but what he did do was to prepare materials for it (I Chronicles 29:1-5). In like manner, that is what the Lord Jesus did when He was on earth. He greatly desired to build the church, and yet all He could do while here was to gather the materials.

Here was a little stone—Peter. A material, as it were, was ready; and when that became evident to Jesus, He revealed a portion of what was in His heart. Said the Lord, "Upon this rock I will build My church." Of course, we know today that the rock is Christ himself, and that rock is Peter's confession concerning Jesus: "You are the Christ, the Son of the living God" (Matthew 16:16). That rock is indeed the Rock of Ages. That rock is not Peter, for he is but a little stone, and a house, we know, cannot be built on a little stone. Therefore, Jesus is himself the Rock, and He will build the church upon himself with living, precious stones, stones that come out of His side—many Peters.

Peter is not the builder but Jesus himself is, for He said, "*I* will build My church." Then, too, it is not Peter's church but it is Christ's church; and in building that church there will be spiritual conflict, for when the spiritual reality comes in, the entire diabolical spiritual world is stirred up: all the gates of Hades will be opened in an attempt to hinder, frustrate, and if possible even destroy the building of the church. In other words, there is a spiritual battle going on throughout the spiritual realm because this church is in the heart of God and of His Christ. Let us never forget, however, that though all the gates of Hades be opened, they shall not prevail against the church. It shall overcome because it is the Lord Jesus who builds the church and He builds it upon himself and with His own life. We see here, then, that in this interaction with Peter and the other disciples Jesus revealed a little something of what the church is.

Church Problems: How They Are to be Resolved

Jesus next revealed, as recorded in Matthew 18, that because human beings are to be involved in His building of the church, there are inevitably going to be problems (vv.15-20). We often hear it said that this or that person is looking for a perfect church; but as long as that person is there, it cannot be perfect. Yes, it is quite true that the Lord Jesus declared: "I will build My church upon this rock and the gates of Hades shall not prevail against it; all the powers of darkness cannot prevail against it." However, it is equally true that you and I are involved in His church; so that whenever there are brethren—both male and female—there will be problems. And hence, if your brother sins against you, what will you do? Will the problem be resolved on the basis of an eye for an eye, a tooth for a tooth? Or will you say, "I will endure, let it go; but I will remember it"? How *do* you solve the problems that are bound to arise in the church? Let it be understood that Jesus made it clear, in so many words here in this lengthy Matthew 18 passage, that all *the problems in the church are to be solved by love and prayer.* Through love and prayer, every problem in the church can be solved: "For where two or three are gathered together in My name, there am I in the midst of them" (see v.20).

The Church Fully Revealed to the Apostles and Prophets

Now that is about all which Jesus revealed while on earth concerning the church. Then He went to the cross: "It is finished." He rose from the dead, ascended on high, and sent the Holy Spirit to this earth. It is by the Holy Spirit that the mystery of the church—that is to say, the mystery of the Christ—was now to be fully revealed to the apostles and the prophets (Ephesians 3:1-10). Only after Jesus' ascension and with the coming of the Holy Spirit did the whole secret come out. Revelation was given to the apostles and prophets by the Holy Spirit.

The Apostle Paul's Vision

For example, on the road to Damascus Saul of Tarsus (later to become the apostle Paul) received a heavenly vision:

> But as he was journeying, it came to pass that he drew near to Damascus; and suddenly there shone round about him a light out of heaven, and falling on the earth he heard a voice saying to him, Saul, Saul, why dost thou persecute me? And he said, Who art thou, Lord? And he said, I am Jesus, whom thou persecutest (Acts 9:3-5).

Saul had seen "the Christ"; indeed, because of this revelatory vision, he understood that the church was the body of Christ: he saw that in his having persecuted the church, he had actually been persecuting the Lord Jesus. And Paul would testify long afterwards before King Agrippa that he had not been disobedient to this heavenly vision (Acts 26:12-19).

The Apostle Peter's Vision

Also, on Simon the tanner's rooftop in Joppa Peter while in a trance saw a vision of a sheet coming down from heaven with all unclean animals, and heard a voice saying, "Peter, rise, kill, and eat." Peter said, "Not so, Lord; I have never eaten anything unclean." And the voice responded: "What God has cleansed, let no man call unclean." Three times the voice had to speak thus; for Peter was very stubborn. And the sheet went back up. This was none other than a revelation of the church; for the church is that which comes down from heaven, touches the earth, and will return to heaven because its nature is heavenly; and yet, all those unclean animals are mentioned. Are we not those unclean animals? Nevertheless, God has cleansed us, and what God has cleansed, let no man say that such is unclean. Through that vision God also said to Peter, "Eat." Let it be understood that *eat* in the Scriptures points to having fellowship. "Fellowship!" said God, as it were, to Peter. But Peter said, "Oh no, I cannot fellowship with the Gentiles." But God made clear to the apostle that "there are neither Jews nor Gentiles, but all are one in Christ" (see Galatians 3:28). All this was revelation to Peter (Acts 10:5-17a, 26-28, 44-46; 11:5-10).

The Apostle John's Vision

The apostle John was on the island of Patmos, exiled there for the word of God and for the testimony of Jesus (Revelation 1:9). On a clear day the outline of the landmass on the other side of the Aegean Sea could be seen. The seven churches of Asia Minor were located there, and it is believed by church historians that before he was exiled, he had ministered to those churches. On one particular Lord's day (1:10a), he was sitting there looking across the water, no doubt thinking about those

The Mystery of Christ

churches because they were on his heart. Then he heard a voice. He turned back and saw a vision—seven golden lampstands with the Son of man walking in the midst of the lampstands (1:12-13). In that vision, God showed him what the churches are.

The churches are golden lampstands, made of pure gold. In the Jerusalem temple and the wilderness tabernacle of old, things were made of wood and overlaid with gold. But the lampstand therein was made entirely of pure gold with no wood involved. Whereas wood in God's word represents humanity, gold betokens divine life. In other words, in the mind of God the church is that which is made up purely of the divine life of Christ. No human flesh is to intervene in the form of foreign particles in that spiritual body. To the contrary, all our flesh—both good and bad—has to be dealt with to preclude its intervention. The church is made of pure gold that has been beaten after much work has been done upon it by means of the cross.

Now the church is to be a lampstand. Yet let us be clear that a lampstand is not an end; it is a means to an end—to shed light. Hence, the church, too, is not an end; it is only the means to an end. And that end or purpose is to lift up light, and the light is Christ. So John beheld the Lord Jesus walking in the midst of the seven lampstands. He is as the High Priest, indeed as a *kingly* High Priest, ministering to the churches and restoring the fallen churches back to himself. It, too, was a vision and revelation of the church.

Once the Holy Spirit had come, the concept of what the church actually is was fully revealed. We therefore now have from the Bible the full revelation of God's concept of the church. What we thus need to do is to read it, assimilate it, and obey it.

Dear heavenly Father, we do praise and thank Thee that just as Christ was conceived in Thy heart before the foundation of the world, so hast Thou also conceived for Christ the church, which is His body. Our Father, as we think of how faithful has been Thy Christ, fully fulfill Thy concept our prayer is that we may not fail in what Thou hast planned for us. Our Father, we do pray that Thou wilt continue to open our understanding in order that we may know what the church really is and what its life should be, so that we may please Thy heart and that Thy will may be done in the church as it has been done in Christ. We ask in the precious name of our Lord Jesus. Amen.

Chapter Two

THE BIRTH OF THE CHURCH

Matthew 16:18—And I also, I say unto thee that thou art Peter, and on this rock I will build my [church], and hades' gates shall not prevail against it.

Acts 1:6-9—They therefore, being come together, asked him saying, Lord, is it at this time that thou restorest the kingdom to Israel? And he said to them, It is not yours to know times or seasons, which the Father has placed in his own authority; but ye will receive power, the Holy Spirit having come upon you, and ye shall be my witnesses both in Jerusalem, and in all Judaea and Samaria, and to the end of the earth. And having said these things he was taken up, they beholding him, and a cloud received him out of their sight.

Acts 1:12-14—Then they returned to Jerusalem from the mount called the mount of Olives, which is near Jerusalem, a sabbath-day's journey off. And when they were come into the city, they went up to the upper chamber, where were staying both Peter, and John, and James, and Andrew, Philip and Thomas, Bartholomew and Matthew, James son of Alphaeus, and Simon the zealot, and Jude the brother of James. These gave themselves all with one accord to continual prayer, with several women, and Mary the mother of Jesus, and with his brethren.

Now We See the Church

> *Acts 2:1-4—And when the day of Pentecost was now accomplishing, they were all together in one place. And there came suddenly a sound out of heaven as of a violent impetuous blowing, and filled all the house where they were sitting. And there appeared to them parted tongues, as of fire, and it sat upon each one of them. And they were all filled with the Holy Spirit, and began to speak with other tongues as the Spirit gave to them to speak forth.*

We will recall that when Jesus was on earth, He once said to Peter: "You are Peter, a stone. I will build My church upon *this* rock." Peter had just confessed Christ as the Son of the living God, and on the basis of that confession, which the Lord likened to a massive rock, Jesus further said, "I will build My church with you, a stone, and with many other living stones." Who is the builder of the church of God? Jesus declares, "*I* will build My church."

From Hebrews 11:10 we learn that Abraham was looking forward to a city with foundations, whose architect and builder is God. So we are told that the church—that city with foundations—is planned and built by none other than God himself.

Then we know that the Holy Spirit is the Spirit of wisdom and understanding, of counsel and might, and He is also the One who builds the church. When Jesus came into this world, it was by the overshadowing of the Holy Spirit over the womb of Mary that He took upon himself a physical body. So it is the Holy Spirit who gave the body to our Lord Jesus, and in the same way, it is the Holy Spirit who has given birth to the church, the body of Christ.

So the church is built by none other than the Triune God himself: the Father purposed it, the Son prepared it, and the Holy Spirit performs it. Therefore, the product is a "holy thing" (cf. Luke 1:35b). I do hope we shall never forget that the church is the work of God; it is not the work of man. Even as the concept of the church is divine in origin, so too is the building of the church: it is a holy building, and it is therefore the work of God.

Wait for the Promise of the Father

After the Lord Jesus rose from the dead He appeared to His disciples for forty days, and then He led them to the Mount of Olives. Even at that moment His disciples, being Jews, were still thinking of the restoration of the nation of Israel. They saw that Jesus had risen from the dead, having overcome death. All power and authority in heaven and on earth were now given to Him (Matthew 28:18b), so naturally they thought it must be the time He would restore the kingdom of Israel. But Jesus had something far, far greater in mind than just restoring the nation of Israel. It is true that one day, in God's time, the nation of Israel *will* be restored to prominence; but before that happens, a greater kingdom, the kingdom of heaven, the kingdom of the Son of God's love (Colossians 1:13b) must be built. So, the risen Lord Jesus told His disciples to wait in Jerusalem until they received the promise of the Father; they would receive power and be His witnesses commencing in Jerusalem, then through all Judea and Samaria, and ultimately to the ends of the earth. Hence, from the time of Jesus' ascension to heaven until His return again to the earth, what He wants His followers to be occupied with is this heavenly kingdom; that we should be His witnesses everywhere concerning it.

So 120 of His disciples returned from the Mount of Ascension to Jerusalem. They went to the Upper Room. There they continued with one accord in prayer for ten whole days (from Passover to Pentecost = 50 days, less the risen Jesus' 40 days of appearing to his disciples = 10 days), waiting for the promise of the Father. And accordingly, on that day of Pentecost the church was born.

The Law of Birth

Before we go further into the history of the church's birth I think we first need to consider together a very basic universal law, in this case, the law of birth. What is the law of birth? It is the law of travail. If there is no travail, there can be no birth. In Genesis 3 God is recorded as saying to the woman: "I will greatly increase your travail in pregnancy—with pain you shall bear children" (see v.16a-b). This was said after the fall of man; but it seems to me that before the Fall this law was already there; that is to say, that without travail, there can be no birth. However, after sin came into the world, God's judgment upon the woman was that the travail would now be painful.

The Travail of God the Son for the Church

It is clear from Scripture that it was because of the travail of God's Son that the church was born. When Jesus came into this world, He was in travail when He emptied himself and took upon himself the fashion of a man, even the form of a slave (Philippians 2:7). He travailed when He went down into the baptismal waters at the river Jordan to take, in our stead as it were, the place of a sinner (Matthew 3:13). Indeed, Jesus travailed throughout His life. He travailed in the Garden of Gethsemane, for there, we are told, His sweat was as great drops of blood falling down upon the ground (Luke 22:44). He travailed greatly on Calvary's cross for He had cried out, "My God, my God, why hast Thou forsaken me?" (Matthew 27:4b) To make sure that He was now dead on the cross, a soldier thrust his spear into His side and out came blood and water. The apostle John witnessed it and testified: "What I witnessed is true. I saw blood and water coming out from deep in His side—out, as it were, from His broken heart" (see John 19:34-35). It is the blood of Jesus which cleanses us from all our sins, and it is His life that was poured out like water which gives us new life; and it is with these—that which came out of Him—that

God builds the church. And hence, as the Scriptures tell us, Jesus shall see the fruit of the travail of His soul and He shall be satisfied (Isaiah 53:11a).

The Travail of God the Father for the Church

We cannot forget, however, that it was not only God the Son who travailed with pain for the birth of the church; we know also that God the Father travailed as much as the Son. How could He forsake His only begotten Son? That communion between the Father and the Son was from all eternity, and there was not a moment—not a single second—of interruption, not even when the Son came upon this earth. On earth Jesus once said, "My Father is with Me, and I always please the Father" (see John 8:29b,c; 16:32b). Yet, because He loves us, God was willing, for our sakes, to forsake His Son and even to crush Him there on the cross. No wonder that from twelve noon to three o'clock that day the sun was darkened (Matthew 27:45), as though the Father had hidden His face so He would not see His Son crushed to death. We cannot imagine how the Father travailed with pain for the birth of the church.

The Travail of God the Holy Spirit for the Church

On that historic day of Pentecost there was a very strong wind blowing, and in the original Greek New Testament it reads that it was a hard breathing. It was as though God the Holy Spirit was travailing in birth by His hard breathing; and through that hard breathing the church was born. Not only is the church a divine concept from all eternity; it is also the work of God the Father, the Son, and the Holy Spirit. Therefore, it is a "holy thing" (cf Luke 1:35c). So we must remember that for the birth of the church to have occurred, every member of the Trinitarian Godhead had to travail in pain to bring it about.

The Travail of Those in the Upper Room

When Jesus was on earth there were far more than 120 disciples. We know this to be true for on one occasion the risen Lord had appeared to 500 brethren together (I Corinthians 15:6a); but only 120 of them gathered in that Upper Room in obedience to the Lord's command, not passively but actively waiting. With one accord, they continually prayed for ten days. What is the picture we see here? We see not only the travail of God, but in sympathetic response to God, 120 believers took it upon themselves to travail for that which God was after. It was through the travailing prayer of those 120 believers that the result of that Pentecost day came to us, for on that day those 120 believers were baptized with the Holy Spirit into one body (I Corinthians 12:13a).

The Law of Birth: to Be Applied to Every Church Birth

The law of birth is the law of travail. This was not only true with the birth of the first church on earth back in the first century; it is a principle which must likewise be applied to the birth of every church of God that will have appeared throughout the ages and throughout the earth. If it is by birth, it has to come with travail. The church is not something organized but must be born, and in order for a church to be born there must be travail. There must be some saints in whatever location on the earth who must have received and taken upon themselves that burden from God and must have begun to travail for the birth of the church, and through their travailing prayer God answered with the birth of a church there. So I hope we see from the very outset that the church is something glorious. It comes forth in glory, but that glory is preceded by travail.

The Wonder of Pentecost

On the day of Pentecost, while the 120 disciples were praying together, preparing themselves and waiting for the promise of the Father, suddenly, there was a hard breathing—a blowing filled the room—and tongues like fire fell upon each of the 120 there. They were filled with the Holy Spirit and began to speak in tongues, speaking of the great things of God (Acts 2:11b).

We usually think of Pentecost in terms of sound and sight. We are more attracted by that which is phenomenal. Moreover, we are interested in what is individual. So when we consider Pentecost, that is usually the way we approach the event. We think of the sound—a wind blowing; we think of the sight—tongues like fire falling; we think of that which is phenomenal—speaking in tongues; and we think of that which is individual—each one was filled with the Holy Spirit and spoke of the great things of God. Now all these facets of the event were true, but Pentecost is much more than that. We need to understand the actual, not just the phenomenal. We need to enter into the real, not only the external. The deeper wonder of Pentecost does not lie in those phenomenal aspects of sound and sight; instead, the wonder of Pentecost is that God did something tremendous, great, marvelous, and glorious. What is the real meaning of Pentecost? What did God actually do on that day?

I believe that those 120 believers must have begun to move from the Upper Room, perhaps to the Porch of Solomon, which was a large place, because that was where the disciples in the early days following Pentecost usually met. The rumors had gone out and begun to spread (2:6a), and it seemed as though much of the city had come together (2:6b); so that the Upper Room was too small for what followed. Evidently, they must have moved to a larger place like Solomon's Porch, and there Peter stood up with the Eleven and delivered the first gospel message (2:14ff.). He first explained the phenomenon that had happened because the people were wondering aloud about it, for some had even said those believers were drunk with new wine. To which Peter responded: "No; this is early morning, it is only 9:00 o'clock; that cannot be the reason for what has occurred" (2:14-15). What, then, was the reason? Peter therefore set about explaining the meaning of Pentecost.

The Baptism with the Holy Spirit Revealed Two Things

> *Having therefore been exalted by the right hand of God, and having received of the Father the promise of the Holy Spirit, he has poured out this which ye behold and hear. (Acts 2:33)*

Revealed That Jesus Is Lord

What happened was a result of the exaltation of the Lord Jesus. When the risen and ascended Jesus was exalted to the right hand of the Father, He received from God the Father the promise of the Holy Spirit, and so He poured Him out.

> *Let the whole house of Israel therefore know assuredly that God has made him, this Jesus whom ye have crucified, both Lord and Christ. (Acts 2:36)*

When you connect verses 33 and 36 together (verses 34 and 35 are parenthetical in character), you can clearly see the meaning of the outpouring of the Holy Spirit. It unveils the fact that God has made Jesus both Lord and Christ. That is part of the deeper meaning of this Pentecost event. The Holy Spirit came down to testify to one particular fact: that Jesus is Lord, that He is Lord of all the earth and is the Christ, the anointed One, who has accomplished what God had sent Him to the earth to do. He is not only the Savior, He is also the Christ, the Anointed High Priest. The Holy Spirit came forth to exalt Jesus, for God the Father has made Jesus the Son both Lord and Christ; and by the Holy Spirit we are to recognize His Lordship: He is the Head, the only Head of the universe. But equally important for those 120 believers and for us today, Jesus Christ is their and our Head; He is the Head of the church. Yet, all that is but one side of Pentecost and what was revealed by the baptism with the Holy Spirit.

The other side is explained in I Corinthians 12:13, because we realize that the New Testament Epistles explain the history contained in the four Gospels and the book of Acts.

Revealed That All Are Baptized into One Body

> *For also in the power of one Spirit we have all been baptised into one body, whether Jews or Greeks, whether bondmen or free, and have all been given to drink of one Spirit. (I Corinthians 12:13)*

The baptism with the Holy Spirit reveals two truths—indeed, two facts. One is that it reveals to us that Jesus is Lord. He is Lord of all—the only Lord, the only King, the only Head. It also reveals to us that in one Spirit we were all baptized into one body and were all made to drink of one Spirit. First, there is brought into view the Head, and then there is the body.

The 120 in the Upper Room were the elite, the cream of Jesus' harvest of disciples. The eleven apostles who had been with Jesus for over three years were there. The other brothers among the 120 who had followed the Lord from the day of John the Baptist until the taking up of Jesus to heaven were also there. Some women were there, too, including the mother of Jesus; and even the brothers of Jesus, according to the flesh, were there (Acts 1:13-14) (We will recall that during Jesus' life on earth, they had not believed in Him (John 7:5); but after His death and resurrection, they were all converted and trusted in Him).

Each one of the 120 had therefore had some personal history with the Lord Jesus. We would say today that those 120 were good Christians, the elite core of Jesus' disciples, and they were very devoted to Him. They were even able to gather together with one accord, despite the fact that it is very difficult for even 20 people to gather in such a way! If these 120 believers were of one accord for only one minute, it might be possible; but for ten days, giving themselves to continual prayer, such is humanly impossible. This congregation of 120 members did not simply pray for five minutes, but the atmosphere was one of continual prayer for ten whole days!

I believe any pastor would greatly desire to have such a congregation; yet let it be recognized that it was exactly that: only a congregation, merely a gathering together of 120 members. There was still no organic growing together. And hence, exactly because it *was* no more than a congregation, those members could, on the one hand, gather together; but on the other hand, they could just as well scatter. In other words, this gathered congregation of 120 individual members was not *organically* united. So that, the wonder of Pentecost is that on that day, in one Spirit, these 120 were baptized into one body. They were no longer a congregation of 120 members; they became a *body* with 120 members. Do we see the difference? The one is only an outward coming together; the other is a being inwardly united into one.

"And they were all made to drink of one Spirit." The Holy Spirit not only came *upon* them and gave them power to be witnesses, but He also came *into* them and thus they were all made to drink of one Spirit. *That* was Pentecost.

We often view the work of the Holy Spirit as that of convicting us of sin, of righteousness, and of judgment (John 16:8-11). We also view the Holy Spirit as the One who begets us—"He that is born of the Spirit is spirit." But do we realize that when we believe in the Lord Jesus we not only are *born of the Spirit*, but simultaneously we also are *baptized in the Spirit into one body*?

The deeper meaning of Pentecost is that of both the Headship of Christ and the body of Christ. No one can separate the Head from the body nor the body from the Head. We first have to see the Head, and then we come to realize we are His body. So the wonder of Pentecost is that on that long-ago day, the risen Jesus took upon himself a corporate body, and in that corporate body He continues to do and to teach. And that, in summary, is the history of the life of the church.

Relationship with the Head

I mentioned before that we too often think only in terms of individuals; but if we can enter into the full purpose of God, we will come to see that though, individually, we are saved, God has made all of us who believe into one body. Yes, it is quite true that no other person can be saved for each of us. Each one of us must repent, believe in the Lord Jesus, and be saved. As an individual believer we need to seek to grow personally, having a personal relationship with the Lord Jesus. All that is important; but let us realize that God has done something far greater than simply saving and maturing the individual Christian. On the contrary, He has brought us Christians together and made us one body; in fact, we are members one of another. In other words, there comes into existence a relationship that is not only with the Head but also with one another. I think it is evident that we cannot do without the Lord Jesus who is our Head.

I well remember that when our brother Watchman Nee came back from England, he told us of his visit with the then well-known elderly brother, George Cutting, who wrote *Safety, Certainty, and Enjoyment,* a pamphlet which has been used of God to save many people. At the time of brother Nee's visit with him, brother Cutting was in his nineties; and on the day when our brother went to visit him, he was in bed, dozing off most of the time. But from time to time, he would wake up and become alert again. So brother Nee sat by brother Cutting's bed, waiting for him to awaken; and when he finally did so, he told our brother: "I cannot do without the Lord, and He cannot do without me." Then he went back to sleep again.

I believe it is clear that we cannot do without the Lord Jesus. But have we come to realize that He cannot do without us? He needs us just as we need Him. There is a relationship between you and the Lord which is so precious.

Relationship with One Another

But, then, brother Nee expanded upon brother Cutting's statement by saying that not only should we say to the Lord, "I cannot do without You, and thank God, You cannot do without me"; we should also say *to one another*, "I cannot do without you, and you cannot do without me." Why is it that I cannot do without Him and He cannot do without me? It is because He is the Head and I am a part of His body. As a member of His body, how can I do without the Head? But the Head will say, "Well now, how can I do without you? You are one of the members of My body and I therefore cannot express Myself, I cannot find My fulfillment, if I do not have you." And the same thing is true of us brethren in Christ since we are members one of another. Have we come to see that we cannot do without each other?

Just recently I was in a certain place and a few Christian brothers were together. One of them confessed to another brother: "I cannot do without you." But he turned to another brother and candidly said, "I do not have the same feeling about you." It was an honest confession. It touched me very deeply. How often we say to a particular brother or sister, "Yes, we are so close; I cannot do without you." But we may say to ourselves concerning another member of the body of Christ: "I do not

The Birth of the Church

need you; I can go on without you." How sad that is. May God show us what He has done on that long-ago Pentecost day. He has brought us into one body by the Holy Spirit, and we therefore need to come to the realization that we cannot do without one another. We must ask God to bring us to the point where we can honestly and sincerely say, "I cannot do without any brother or sister—in fact, without any and all of my brothers and sisters." And the same thing will be said of me. However small a member I am, the other brothers and sisters will say, "No, you are needed; I need you as well." Such is the wonder of Pentecost. So may the Lord help us.

Dear heavenly Father, we are so grateful that, for the birth of the church, Thou hast travailed with pain. We are so grateful that Thou hast brought us into being as the body of Christ. What a glorious thing is the church, the body of Christ. We do praise and thank Thee that we are in that body. We do acknowledge Thee, our Lord Jesus, as our Head. There is no other Head but Thou Thyself; and we do acknowledge that we are but members, yet members one of another belonging to the same body. Father, we pray that by Thy Holy Spirit Thou wilt bring us into this glorious truth—that we cannot do without Christ as Christ cannot do without us, and likewise, that we cannot do without one another. Lord, bring us to Thy truth so that Thou mayest be able to continue to do and to teach through that body of Thine until, one day, there will be that eternal union. We ask in Thy precious name. Amen.

Chapter Three

THE CHURCH IN JERUSALEM

Acts 1:12-14—Then they returned to Jerusalem from the mount called the mount of Olives, which is near Jerusalem, a sabbath-day's journey off. And when they were come into the city, they went up to the upper chamber, where were staying both Peter, and John, and James, and Andrew, Philip and Thomas, Bartholomew and Matthew, James son of Alphaeus, and Simon the zealot, and Jude the brother of James. These gave themselves all with one accord to continual prayer, with several women, and Mary the mother of Jesus, and with his brethren.

Acts 2:37-47—And having heard it they were pricked in heart, and said to Peter and the other apostles, What shall we do, brethren? And Peter said to them, Repent, and be baptised, each one of you, in the name of Jesus Christ, for remission of sins, and ye will receive the gift of the Holy Spirit. For to you is the promise and to your children, and to all who are afar off, as many as the Lord our God may call. And with many other words he testified and exhorted them, saying, Be saved from this perverse generation. Those then who had accepted his word were baptised; and there were added in that day about three thousand souls.

> *And they persevered in the teaching and fellowship of the apostles, in breaking of bread and prayers. And fear was upon every soul, and many wonders and signs took place through the apostles' means. And all that believed were together, and had all things common, and sold their possessions and substance, and distributed them to all, according as any one might have need. And every day, being constantly in the temple with one accord, and breaking bread in the house, they received their food with gladness and simplicity of heart, praising God, and having favour with all the people; and the Lord added to the [church] daily those that were to be saved.*
>
> *Acts 4:32-33—And the heart and soul of the multitude of those that had believed were one, and not one said that anything of what he possessed was his own, but all things were common to them; and with great power did the apostles give witness of the resurrection of the Lord Jesus, and great grace was upon them all.*

We are considering together the life of the church, the body of Christ. The first church that appeared on earth was the one in Jerusalem. Therefore, I would like for us to observe the life of the church in Jerusalem.

We know there is but one church. Jesus had declared: "On this rock I will build My church, and the gates of Hades shall not prevail against it" (see Matthew 16:18). That is the one church universal; nevertheless, in the building of that one church God does so through the many churches local. This is very evident from what we find in the book of Acts; yet we can also find evidence for this in the book of Revelation. For on the one hand we are shown in the latter book's first three chapters

The Church in Jerusalem

seven local churches in the region of Asia Minor, and on the other hand we are shown in Revelation chapters 21-22 the church universal—also spoken of as the holy city, the new Jerusalem. Hence, we can say that the actual building of the church universal is by means of the building up of all the churches local everywhere on earth. And the first local church to appear on the earth was the one in Jerusalem. It can therefore be said that the church in Jerusalem occupies a very special place in the history of the church.

Now after Jesus had ascended to heaven from the Mount of Olives just outside Jerusalem, some of His disciples returned to the Jewish capital. They went directly to the Upper Room where they obediently waited actively, they praying with one accord for the coming of the promise of the Holy Spirit.

The Bible tells us that in that upper-level chamber there were the twelve apostles (Matthias having replaced Judas Iscariot), and all their names are given (Acts 1:13-14 with 1:23-26). In addition there were some women. Who were these women? From Luke 8:2-3 we learn that while Jesus was continually ministering on the earth there were a number of women who had followed Him and were ministering to Him and His disciples: those such as Mary Magdalene; Joanna, wife of Herod's steward; Susanna; and still other but unnamed women. Most likely, therefore, these were the women who were there in the Upper Room. But the record also specifically states that Mary the mother of Jesus was there along with the flesh-and-blood brethren of the Lord Jesus. It will be remembered that while Jesus was on earth His kinfolk had not believed in Him (John 7:5); but after His death and resurrection, somehow, all His brethren in the flesh became His disciples, and among those of them cited were James and Jude. So all together, there were about 120 believers who were present in the Upper Room.

We can say that these 120 were the cream of all the disciples of Jesus at that time. They were the ones who had faithfully followed the Lord. They were the ones who had now obeyed Him by having returned to Jerusalem and were waiting for the coming of the promised Holy Spirit. They were very well acquainted with the Lord and all of them had a long personal history with Him. And while they all were waiting and travailing in prayer, the Holy Spirit descended from heaven on that day of Pentecost. With the result that they all were filled with the Holy Spirit as well as something further happened: in one Spirit those 120 believers were baptized into one body—the body of Christ (cf. I Corinthians 12:12b-13). Not only did each one of them come into an organic personal relationship with the Lord himself, but they also were organically united one with another as one body. They were no longer 120 individual believers, but they were now 120 members of the one body of Christ.

One People—One Body

In reading the record of what had occurred on that Pentecost day, we most likely think that it was Peter alone who stood up and preached that first gospel message; if you read carefully, however, you learn that when Peter stood up, the other eleven stood up with him (Acts 2:14a). And if you read still more carefully, you learn that it was also the 120. Every one of them spoke in tongues "of the great things of God" (Acts 2:11b), and it was this that drew the multitudes to them. Evidently, at some point in these proceedings they relocated themselves from that limited upper chamber over to Solomon's Porch, since that was a place which could accommodate multitudes of people (cf. Acts 5:12b); and everybody in the crowd heard them speaking in their native language.

Let us therefore notice that immediately after the body was born all the members of that body were functioning. It was not just Peter functioning, not just the eleven apostles functioning with him, but every member in that body—man and woman—was functioning. They were all testifying, speaking of the great things of God, and it drew the multitudes to them. Now *that* is a healthy body. When you see every member of the body functioning, you know that body is healthy. So thank God, from the very beginning a very healthy body was born.

When the multitude heard the preaching of the gospel, they were pricked in heart. It was the time of the Feast of Pentecost and many Jews from all over the world were gathered in Jerusalem to celebrate. Sad to say, many people only came because of tradition; it was a religion to them. But thank God, among the multitude there were some people who were real seekers of God and seekers of truth. It was into the lives of these people that the spiritual light broke. So that when they heard the preaching of the gospel, they were pricked in heart and asked Peter and the eleven apostles: "What should we do? We today see that we have rejected Christ. Now, then, what should we do?"

Peter said, "Repent, and be baptized in the name of the Lord Jesus for the remission of your sins; and you will receive the promise of the Holy Spirit, because the promise is not only to you but to your children, not only to those of you who are near but also to those generations who are far off." Those people received fully the words of Peter. The apostle spoke many other words: he exhorted them to be saved from that current perverse generation who had rejected the Savior, to be separated from them and to be wholly committed to Christ Jesus. So those who believed were baptized, and in one day, some 3,000 souls were added. Those 3,000 were *soundly* saved. Theirs were perfect births.

Too often today, when people say they believe in the Lord Jesus, their faith is not that absolute; it is not that clear. But back then in Jerusalem were a people (a) who repented; (b) who separated themselves from the world—from the perverse generation of that day; (c) who were baptized and fully committed to Christ; and (d) who received the promise of the Holy Spirit and were filled with the Spirit. Without any question they were soundly saved, perfectly born, even though they were only babes in Christ—just as we were when we believed in the Lord Jesus, in that we were babes in Christ at the beginning of our rebirth in Christ. And because they were so soundly saved and perfectly born, therefore, those 3,000 and the 120 were joined together as one body. There was no gap between them of any kind. They simply became one people, one body. That was the church in Jerusalem.

The Jerusalem church was not exclusively composed of "veterans" in Christ Jesus; to the contrary, it was also composed, even from the very beginning, of babes in Christ. To describe this church another way: it was a family. Those who knew the Lord for a long time were able to help those who were babes in Christ, and those who were babes in Christ were humble enough to receive help from those who knew the Lord very well. They merged together as one because they were indeed one—one family, one people, one church, one body.

A New Way of Life

How can there be a new living body and there not be a new way of life? Without any planning, with no need to impose or enforce anything, there began to appear, supernaturally naturally, in the Jerusalem church a lifestyle that was a new way of life. Formerly, they each lived their own lives, but something had happened to alter all that. They had become one people—not only one people but one body; and very quickly, body life began to show forth. Now body life is not something planned or manufactured. Body life comes out of life. These brethren in Christ shared a common life. Because they were in the one body, quite naturally, they began to live out together a way of life and a style of life. It was a way of life that was so natural—a corporate life together that the world had never seen before. It was a way of life which was radically different from all the ways of living that the world could ever know because Jesus himself had become the Way for themselves (cf. John 14:6a).

Body Life

What kind of life is body life? What kind of life did these early believers live out as the church of God? First of all, they devoted themselves continually to—they occupied themselves totally with—the teaching and fellowship of the apostles, the breaking of bread, and prayers (Acts 2:42 Darby, ASV, RSV). Before this Pentecost experience happened, they had been occupied with many other things, but thereafter, what now occupied their lives? How did they live? They continued faithfully, occupying themselves with the teaching and the fellowship of the apostles, the breaking of bread, and prayers. Let us consider more closely each of these elements of their life together.

The Teaching of the Apostles

What exactly is the teaching of the apostles? We should notice that the word teaching is cast here in singular number, whereas the word apostles is in plural number. There were twelve apostles, but there was only one teaching of those twelve apostles. What is the teaching of the apostles? Let us recall what the Lord Jesus had instructed: "Go and disciple the nations, baptizing them in the name of the Father, the Son, and the Holy Spirit; teaching them to obey all things I have commanded you, and I will be with you to the end of the age" (see Matthew 28:19-20). We may therefore say that the teaching of the apostles was none other than what the Lord had taught them. So they simply taught all these new believers what the Lord had taught them.

Let us also recall what the apostle Paul has written: "What I delivered to you was just what I received from the Lord" (see I Corinthians 11:23a). Hence, we see here that the apostles did not have their own teaching; rather, they only taught what they themselves were taught by the Lord. So, the teaching of the apostles is none other than the teaching of Christ. In brief, they taught them Christ.

The Fellowship of the Apostles

The fellowship of the apostles. Again, let us notice that the word fellowship is singular in number here—one fellowship; whereas the word apostles is plural in number—a number of apostles. But what is the fellowship of the apostles? We read in I Corinthians 1:9 that "God is faithful, by whom ye have been called into the fellowship of his Son Jesus Christ our Lord."

And in I John 1:3 we read: "That which we have seen and heard we report to you, that ye also may have fellowship with us; and our fellowship is indeed with the Father, and with his Son Jesus Christ." It is therefore clear that the fellowship of the apostles is none other than the fellowship of God's Son Jesus Christ. Peter did not have his own fellowship; neither did Paul have his own fellowship. Actually, he told those Corinthian believers who had said "I am of Paul" that it was wrong since Christ is not divided (I Corinthians 1:12-13a). There is only one fellowship—the fellowship of God's Son Jesus Christ. The teaching consists of our faith; the fellowship consists of our practice. There is but one faith and one fellowship—one common faith and one common fellowship. So, those people on Pentecost day received the teaching and fellowship of Christ. They were taught of Christ, and they fellowshiped in Christ. They fellowshiped one another with Christ. And that is one aspect of body life.

Breaking of Bread and Prayers

Breaking of bread and prayers. The teaching and fellowship of the apostles are especially expressed in two ways. One is the breaking of bread (also known as the Lord's Table).

Why is it so important? It is because the breaking of bread is our communion with the Lord. We are in communion with His blood, we are in communion with His body, and we are in communion one with another. It is a practical expression of our union and communion in Christ Jesus.

Why also are prayers so important? What is in view here is not personal prayer but corporate prayer, a praying together. This is so important because prayers express our union with Christ in His purpose and interest. We are not merely praying each one for ourselves or for our small circles; rather, we are praying for His interest and His purpose. So the breaking of bread is actually the life of the church, and prayer is the ministry of the church.

How important and how essential it is that we are at the Lord's Table! It is not a ritual; it is not a form; it is not a habit; it is not a tradition. Each time we gather together at His Table and remember the Lord, we are in spiritual communion with His blood and with His body, and we are in fellowship with all the brothers and sisters—all the members of the body of Christ—throughout the whole world. It is a testimony; and it is body life. How can you say you have body life if you absent yourself from the Lord's Table? How can you say you have body life if you absent yourself from prayer? These are the practical expressions of the body of Christ and of body life. From the very beginning those 3,120 believers occupied themselves in this manner. As many believers as they were, there were that many at the Lord's Table and that many in corporate prayer. Now that is a further aspect of body life.

Togetherness

Everything Shared Together

All that believed were together. Now this togetherness was more than merely a physical one; this togetherness was a spiritual oneness, and it was expressed in different ways. It was expressed in their concern and care for one another. They were a people who were completely delivered from self-possessiveness. Self-possessiveness is one of the primitive instincts of human beings. Even a child has this instinct of self-possessiveness. When they are playing with their toys, they will say, "This is mine!" or "That is mine!" We are all selfish, self-centered people. Yet, when those 3,120 people were baptized into one body, all that selfishness, all that self-possessiveness vanished. They shared everything. Nobody said, "This is mine." They cared for one another; they supplied the needs of one another because, during those Pentecost days, many had come to celebrate the Feast and did not return to their various homelands. So there were no jobs for these pilgrim Jews who had become Christians; they were not engaged in any work or occupation. So homes were opened for them to live in, they ate together, and they shared everything together.

Let us suppose a cell in your body says, "This cell life is mine." What happens? You come down with cancer. No cell in a healthy body will say, "This is mine"; instead, all the cells in a healthy body share everything with the whole body.

When the Spirit of God gave birth to that heavenly body on earth, its many members began to live a lifestyle never before seen on this earth. Such a lifestyle was not taught nor was it enforced; to the contrary, it was a spiritually natural development. That body's members were continually together and caring for one another. How, then, can we today say we are one body if we do not care for one another?

Breaking Bread from House to House

They also expressed their togetherness by breaking bread from house to house. They loved the Lord so much and they loved one another so much that, probably, at every meal, they just celebrated in remembering the Lord together. I sometimes feel we make this matter of the Lord's Table too complicated. Actually, it should be observed in a very, very simple manner. After a meal, if we feel touched by the grace and love of God, let us break bread and give thanks to the Lord. Those Christians back then did that to show their togetherness.

They Assembled Daily

They assembled daily in the temple with one accord. That, too, is an expression of body life—of togetherness. You cannot say, "My spirit is with you" while at the same time your body is not there. That is not togetherness. On the other hand, if the body is there but your spirit is not, that is not togetherness either. If there is to be togetherness, both your spirit and your body should be there.

Those Pentecost-day believers did not forsake the assembling of the saints (cf. Hebrews 10:25a); rather, they encouraged and exhorted one another to love and good works (Hebrews 10:25b, 24). That is togetherness. Modern life is not conducive to spiritual living, that is true. But in spite of that, I am very much ashamed when I consider how those early believers had lived out body life in contrast to how we live today, supposedly, according to body life. We need to go before the Lord about our failure in this regard.

Delivered from Love of the World

They received their food with gladness and simplicity of heart, praising God and having favour with all the people. I believe that in their having received their food with gladness and simplicity of heart and praising God, it indicated that they were a joyful, thankful, contented people. They were completely delivered from the love of the world. They began to live a simple life. How can we say we are delivered from the world if we still live a very complicated life? A Christian life ought to be very simple. We ought to be content with what the

Lord has given us, completely delivered from the love of the world. A new lifestyle comes forth—a happy, contented, thankful, praising people. I believe wherever and whenever the Spirit of God is truly moving, you will find a people living simply—not for the world, not for themselves, but for the Lord. That is body life; that is the life of the church. So when the world observed those early Christians, they were amazed because they had never witnessed anything like it on the earth.

Humility

The heart and the soul of the multitude that had believed were one. On the day of Pentecost 3,000 souls were added; and Acts chapter 2 further says that the Lord added more believers to the church daily (v.47). Then we read in Acts 4 that the number of believers grew to be 5,000 (v.4). All these people were one in heart and one in mind (v.32 NIV). In their heart was Christ's love; in their mind was the mind of Christ—that of humility, even as the apostle Paul has made known to us in Philippians chapter 2 (vv.5-8). They loved the Lord with their whole heart; they loved one another in humility. They were truly one.

We will recall that Jesus, before He died, prayed, "Father, that they may be one as We are one" (see John 17:21a). That prayer was answered here in the Jerusalem church. There was one many-membered body living out one life, living for Christ, and living for one another. This was the life of the church in Jerusalem.

Consequences of Living Body Life

Great Power Given
When Jesus' Resurrection Is Preached

What are the uplifting consequences of living such a life? Acts 4:33 informs us that "with great power did the apostles give witness of the resurrection of the Lord Jesus ..." One positive consequence is that with great power the apostles gave witness to the resurrection of the Lord Jesus. Jesus' resurrection is one of the cardinal points of our Christian faith. I Corinthians 15:3-4 describes the matter this way: that Christ died for us, He was buried, and He was resurrected. These three facts are the very essence of the gospel. We read in the book of Acts that whenever the gospel was preached, the resurrection of the Lord Jesus was always mentioned. His resurrection is more than simply an historical fact; nor is it just a doctrine, a teaching. Jesus' resurrection is a reality in that believers live out His resurrection life. Therefore, when the apostles preached the resurrection, they preached with great power.

Oftentimes today we preach without power. We may preach the resurrection of the Lord Jesus, but people do not believe because they say they do not see it. Indeed, resurrection life that is lived out is a life that the world has never seen. It is life out of death, overcoming death. And if people can see it expressed in the life of the believers and then someone among them preaches the resurrection of the Lord Jesus, it no longer remains only a doctrine or historical fact; it has become a spiritual reality. There is power associated with it. Hence, the consequence of living body life is that it bestows great power upon our witnessing.

Great Grace Given by God

A second positive consequence of body life being expressed is that "great grace was upon them all." This people in the Jerusalem church received great grace from God. Or to put it another way, because these believers lived as a body, therefore, the fullness of the Head was with them. That is great grace.

Fear Comes upon Both Church and World

We find yet another consequence mentioned in Acts 2: "And fear was upon every soul" (v.43a). This is again mentioned in Acts 5:11: "And great fear came upon all the [church], and upon all who heard these things." If we use another word for fear here it will probably bring out the meaning more clearly—the word awe. There was an awesomeness which came upon the entire church because everything was so real: the Lord was real; the Holy Spirit was real; every spiritual aspect was intensely real. Now when everything is so real, will there not descend upon you and me that sense of awe? When we stand before God, there is an awe present; indeed, whenever you and I sense the presence of the Lord, there is an awe which comes over us. We can perhaps call it fear, a holy fear.

Where is that fear today? Certainly if confronted by true body life in the church, fear will come to the world because it encounters something that is so awesome, so heavenly, so living, and so real. But fear also comes upon the church—upon all those who are the Lord's. We who are in the church live a life of awe and fear. We dare not do anything casually or in the flesh because the Lord is here among us. And such, too, can be said to be the consequence of living the body life.

The Lord Adds to the Church

A final positive consequence of body life is that the Lord added to the church daily "those that were to be saved" (Acts 2:47). Many in the world were touched by the church believers' very lives, and thus the unbelievers in the world were drawn to the Lord. Such, then, were the varied uplifting consequences of the body life of the church in Jerusalem.

Problems

Ananias and Sapphira

Did the saints in the Jerusalem church have problems? Most certainly. As long as we are in the flesh and as long as we *give in* to the flesh, the Enemy will always have ground to attack. It is inevitable that when the Lord is working, the Enemy will also be working; for as we shall see, the Enemy worked through the flesh of Ananias and Sapphira.

Now as we have just considered together, the church in Jerusalem began in such a glorious way. Indeed, it was a most glorious time: people were delivered from themselves; people who had means sold their possessions from time to time and lay the resulting funds at the feet of the apostles as their way of sharing with others who were in need (Acts 4:34b-35). Yet, there was nothing forced or imposed, nothing preached. It was all done voluntarily, out of a heart of love. Oh, how glorious it in fact was!

But then there were Ananias and Sapphira—who succumbed to vainglory. The entire incident can be found in Acts 4:36-5:11. They had observed how the Levite, Joseph from Cyprus, had sold his land and had brought all the money from the sale to the apostles. Most likely when he did this he, as it were, was praised by the apostles for having done this act of charity, because they now called him Barnabas—meaning, the

Son of Encouragement or Consolation. Somehow, all this generosity and resultant praise stirred up something within this couple: "We too want that praise, we also want that glory." But in their case it turned out to be vainglory. In the world people want to gain something; but in the church, what are you going to gain? For the church—if it is an expression of the true church—is a place for loss, not for gain. You do not go to the church to *gain* something; you go there to *give* something. What can you get in the church? What can the church offer to you? Nothing. Yet somehow, when people's flesh is active, even in the church people are out to gain some vainglory.

So what occurred was that Ananias and Sapphira sold a piece of their property. It soon became evident that on the one hand, they wanted to gain some glory; but on the other hand, they could not let go of the world completely. They had not needed to do this, for had they not done so, nobody would have said anything; but their fleshly desire had become so great that they wanted to have the benefit of both worlds: praise in the church and continued pleasures of the world. Hence, they kept back some of the land-sale money, gave part to the church, and pretended to convey the notion that what they placed at the apostles' feet was everything attained from the sale. *However*, they forgot that the Holy Spirit was in the church. For Peter said to Ananias: "Why do you deceive the Holy Spirit? Before you sold the property, it was yours; and even after you sold it, it was still yours to dispose of the funds as you would wish. Why do you lie to the Holy Spirit?" And with that, the Spirit's discipline came swiftly and severely upon both Ananias and his wife.

We thank God for this incident having been recorded because it teaches us a number of things. Do we really believe that the Holy Spirit is in the church? Or is it just a teaching? If we truly believe the Holy Spirit is in the church, then it is not a matter of only living before man; it is a matter of living also before God. We believe in the Holy Spirit. We believe the Holy Spirit is present in the church. If that is the case, do you think we should honor Him? Or do you think we can deceive Him? Should we quench Him, grieve Him, cheat Him? I think that is a lesson we need to learn.

Also, through this incident we come to see and understand discipline. A church cannot be built without discipline. We do not like discipline. We want freedom, liberty. We want to do whatever we want and to do it in our own way. We may think the church is a democracy and that everybody can thus do whatever he likes or wants. No; the church is not a democracy; it is a theocracy. The Lord is King. So there is discipline. Let us realize here that it was not Peter who disciplined Ananias and Sapphira; it was the Holy Spirit who did it. Peter was but an instrument. We need to see that.

In the church, if some brothers in responsibility begin to exercise some discipline towards us, we may think that it is *they* who are disciplining us. If we interpret it that way, there is doubtless a rebellious spirit which is rising in us; but we need to see that discipline in the church comes from the Holy Spirit and not from man because in the church the Holy Spirit represents Christ the Head of the church. So let us learn to believe in discipline and to accept it.

We also need to realize that problems are not necessarily negative or destructive in character. Problems, if they are handled well, can be disguised blessings; and because of this or that problem, we discover that discipline is actually a blessing.

"And fear came upon all the [church]" (Acts 5:11a). Let us realize that love and fear are not opposites; instead, they complement each other. We may sometimes think that if it is love, there should be no fear present. It is quite true that Scripture tells us that perfect love casts out fear (I John 4:18a). The fear in view there, however, is that of punishment, not the fear of displeasing the Lord. If you love the Lord, there is always a fear there: you are afraid you may displease Him. So this case with Ananias and Sapphira, which is a very sad case, exhibits the fact that in the body of Christ, there is—and there must be—discipline. That is a part of body life.

Hellenistic Widows

As the numbers in the church at Jerusalem began to grow, another problem arose. It and its solution is laid out in some detail in Acts 6:1-6. Those widows among the Greek-speaking or Hellenistic Jews were being neglected in the daily distribution of food towards them. Life was understandably hard at that time, and apparently there were many widows in the church as a whole. Some of them were those who had come from outside Jerusalem and/or outside of Judea; they were Hellenistic Jews who had been living among the Jewish Dispersion scattered throughout the Gentile cities within the Roman Empire. On the other hand, there were the Hebrew Jews who were those who lived in Judea. The Hellenistic Jews soon discovered that the daily supply of food towards their widows was being overlooked, and because of that there was murmuring.

The Enemy always uses murmuring to damage or even destroy the church. What happens too often is that if you have any complaint—if you see anything missing or lacking—you do not go to the responsible brothers and tell them openly. That is what you ought to do, but instead of doing that, you murmur behind their backs. And if you allow it to grow, that murmuring will ultimately sow discord and may even result in rebellion. This very consequence can be found in the Old Testament with respect to the children of Israel.

As a matter of fact, however, this neglect among the saints in the Jerusalem church had not been intentional; it had been circumstantial in nature because at that time the apostles had been doing everything. They had not only been ministering the word of God, they also had been the ones serving the meal tables. With thousands and thousands of believers in the church, how could twelve people take care of all of them and do it well? It was humanly impossible. Furthermore, all the apostles were Hebrew Jews, and hence they were not familiar with the conditions of the Hellenistic Jews. Therefore, their widows were being neglected, yet not intentionally; it was simply a matter of circumstance. The Hellenistic brothers and sisters should have known of this situation and gone to the apostles and told them of the problem and should have tried to help them solve it. But instead of doing that, they murmured behind the apostles' backs; it exhibits the fact that they distrusted them.

When the murmuring got louder and louder, it eventually came to the ears of the apostles. Thank God, those apostles, instead of getting angry, humbled themselves before all the brothers and sisters, gathered all the brethren of the church together, and acknowledged that, "Yes, here is a serious problem among us all; let's solve it together. All you brethren can choose seven in the church to take care of the meal tables so that we can devote ourselves solely to preaching and to prayer." So the church chose seven brothers from among all the saints. And it turned out that all but one of the seven were Hellenistic Jews, and even that one was a Gentile proselyte convert to Judaism from Antioch. Here we see that the majority in the Jerusalem church, all of whom were probably Hebrew Jews, loved the minority so much that they chose all seven from among the minority. They definitely wanted the Hellenistic widows to be taken care of, and so they were not afraid if their *own* widows might be neglected. That was a sign of great love—even the love of Christ.

Thus, it can be seen that the result of this particular problem was that the Lord used this situation to show the church that there must be division of labor. Nobody can do everything. Nobody can dominate. Every brother and sister has his or her service to contribute; and further, as a consequence of this division of labor God greatly blessed the Jerusalem church. For we learn from the Biblical record of this problem and its solution that much blessing immediately followed (Acts 6:7). Hence, problems are not bad; problems are opportunities.

Persecution

All the brothers and sisters in the church at Jerusalem were together and were so happy. True church life is so happy; body life is so joyful. And they went on together like that for seven years. Those from among the Dispersion did not want to go back to their homelands anymore; they instead wanted to stay in Jerusalem. They had forgotten Jesus' command: "Go from Jerusalem to Judea to Samaria and to the ends of the earth" (see Acts 1:8). They were so happy and contented living together that they forgot the Lord's commission to His disciples (see again Matthew 28:19-20).

Accordingly, what did the Lord do? He allowed persecution to break out (Acts 8:1b). Now that constituted yet another problem, for persecution came to the church in Jerusalem; but thank God, through that persecution, all the believers were scattered throughout the whole known world of that day; and they therefore brought the gospel to the world in fulfillment of the command of the Lord. So problems are not necessarily bad. God sometimes allows persecution as a catalyst for spreading His word. After all the believers left Jerusalem only the apostles remained (see again Acts 8:1b); but very soon, they had the same number of believers in the Jerusalem church (Acts 9:31 mgn). Such was the life of the church in Jerusalem. I pray we shall learn a great deal from it.

Dear Lord, we do praise and thank Thee that Thou dost show us Thy body as it first appeared on earth. What a life—Your life shown and expressed in and through a people as one. Lord, our hearts do long for that. We cry to Thee: Make us what Thou dost want us to be so that Thou mayest be glorified. In Thy precious name we pray. Amen.

Chapter Four

THE CHURCH IN ANTIOCH

Acts 11:19-30—*They then who had been scattered abroad through the tribulation that took place on the occasion of Stephen, passed through the country to Phoenicia and Cyprus and Antioch, speaking the word to no one but to Jews alone. But there were certain of them, Cyprians and Cyrenians, who entering into Antioch spoke to the Greeks also, announcing the glad tidings of the Lord Jesus. And the Lord's hand was with them, and a great number believed and turned to the Lord. And the report concerning them reached the ears of the [church] which was in Jerusalem, and they sent out Barnabas to go through as far as Antioch: who, having arrived and seeing the grace of God, rejoiced, and exhorted all with purpose of heart to abide with the Lord; for he was a good man and full of the Holy Spirit and of faith; and a large crowd of people were added to the Lord. And he went away to Tarsus to seek out Saul. And having found him, he brought him to Antioch. And so it was with them that for a whole year they were gathered together in the [church] and taught a large crowd: and the disciples were first called Christians in Antioch.*

Now in these days prophets went down from Jerusalem to Antioch; and one from among them, by name Agabus, rose up and signified by the Spirit that there was going to be a great famine over all the inhabited earth, which also came to pass under Claudius. And they determined, according as any one of the disciples was well off, each of them to send to the brethren who dwelt in Judaea, to minister to them; which also they did, sending it to the elders by the hand of Barnabas and Saul.

It was mentioned previously that the church is not that which was conceived by man but was conceived by God before the foundation of the world. If we want to know what the church is meant to be, we cannot only look to history; we need also to look into the word of God. We must find out what was originally in God's mind concerning the church. The success or failure of the church is therefore not to be measured by man but is to be measured by how near it is in every respect to God's concept of what the church is meant to be.

We need to be reminded again that Jesus said, "I will build My church." And hence, the church is not that which man can build but it is Christ who builds it. Moreover, the church is universal in scope, for it includes all God's people: from the first of those who out from the unbelieving world believed in the Lord Jesus to those very last who shall have done so. The church is thus universal—and, it is one. Yet the way God builds His church is by establishing churches in every locality upon the earth. The first one that was established was the church in Jerusalem, but that was just the beginning. It was not the end because we will recall that Jesus had also said: "You shall be My witnesses beginning from Jerusalem, then through Judaea and Samaria, and unto the ends of the earth" (Acts 1:8). We see, then, that God is building the church by establishing His churches locally everywhere upon the earth as long as the age of grace continues. Let us briefly review what we learned last time how that first church at Jerusalem had come into being.

The Church in Antioch

Reviewing the History of the First Church

In the Jerusalem church's beginning there were only 120 believers—those who had followed the Lord Jesus and were faithful to Him while He was on earth. They had gathered in the Upper Room, had prayed together, and had waited for the Holy Spirit to come to them. Then, on the day of Pentecost the Holy Spirit came upon them, and by one Spirit they were baptized into one body (cf. again I Corinthians 12:13a). That was the very beginning of the Lord's church on earth. And thank God, on that very same day 3,000 more souls were added to the Lord and to the church—those, indeed, whose hearts had been pricked and had repented and believed in Jesus. They, too, were baptized and had received the promise of the Holy Spirit. They persevered in the teaching and fellowship of the apostles, in the breaking of bread and in prayers. And, furthermore, we learn that the Lord added even more people to the church on a daily basis (Acts 2:47). However, God was still not finished adding to the Jerusalem church; for after the incident of a cripple having been healed at the temple gate called Beautiful (Acts 3:2), a great multitude gathered together around Peter and John, who preached the gospel to them, resulting in many more having believed in the Lord Jesus. The number of brethren in Jerusalem had therefore increased still further to some 5,000 people (Acts 4:4).

We will also recall the incident revolving around Ananias and Sapphira, with severe discipline having come upon them very swiftly. And because of this, the fear of the Lord fell upon all of God's people; and many more, both men and women, were added to the Lord and to the church because of that incident (Acts 5:11-14).

Continuing with this review, we also learned, from Acts 6, that seven men were appointed to take care of the meal tables so that the apostles could devote themselves to prayer and to the ministry of God's word, and consequently God greatly blessed them. Many more came to the Lord, even many priests (v.7). It has been estimated that by this time the church in Jerusalem must have comprised some 20,000 believers, including women and children. Nevertheless, in spite of such a great number, they were all one; they were all together. They broke bread from house to house, they worshiped the Lord, and they continued in fellowship. Without any doubt the church in Jerusalem had experienced a glorious beginning.

Now the brothers and sisters who were in Jerusalem fellowshiping together were so happy with their fellowship. They were enjoying the Lord and one another so much that somehow they forgot what He had told them: "Go, be My witnesses in Jerusalem, and from Jerusalem to all Judea and Samaria, and even to the ends of the earth." Instead of going forth and spreading the testimony of Jesus throughout the earth, they simply remained together enjoying the Lord and one another.

This state of affairs probably continued for some seven or eight years. Finally, God had to do something, and so He allowed persecution to come upon the church in Jerusalem. It started with the stoning of Stephen (Acts 7:54-8:3), one of the seven brethren who had been serving the meal tables among the saints. Especially under the Pharisee, Saul of Tarsus, the persecution was greatly increased; so much so that all the disciples began to scatter and go elsewhere. They left Jerusalem, leaving only the apostles there, and they went throughout Judea and Samaria (Acts 8:1c). They not only were trying to flee from persecution; actually, it was God who sovereignly sent them out to all Judea and Samaria to preach the gospel (Acts 8:4). So that by the time of Acts 9 all the churches in Judea, Galilee, and Samaria were growing in the Lord and had peace (Acts 9:31). But that was not the end, for this brief review now brings us to the founding of the church at Antioch.

The Church in Antioch

We learn from Acts 11 that some of those who had fled from Jerusalem because of persecution traveled even farther afield. They went by land and sea, to such places as Phoenicia, Cyprus and Antioch. Now Antioch was in Syria; and when the disciples from Jerusalem entered there, they announced the glad tidings of the Lord Jesus. But these Jewish believers who had been scattered forth were still bound by their Judaism, so they spoke only to the Jews who long before this had been dispersed into those foreign lands and cities. Even so, there were also among these scattered saints some Cyprians from the island of Cyprus and Cyrenians from North Africa, who themselves were Gentiles who had been converted to Judaism; and they began to share the gospel not only to those dispersed Jews at Antioch but also to the Gentiles who were there. Let us momentarily pause here to remind ourselves of who all had been at Jerusalem at the time of Jesus' crucifixion and the subsequent Festival of Pentecost.

We will recall that during that time Jews from everywhere both near and far had been present together at the Jewish capital: not only those Jews who currently lived in the Promised Land itself but also those in the Dispersion who were Hellenistic Jews. Also there in the capital were a number of Gentiles who were proselyte converts to Judaism. One such was the man who had helped Jesus bear His cross up the hill of Calvary and whose name was Simon, a Cyrenian (Matthew 27:32). On the other hand, one Hellenistic Jew who was present at Jerusalem at this time was Barnabas, whose name formerly had been Joseph, and who was a Levite from Cyprus (Acts 4:36-37). So we learn from the Scriptures that present in Jerusalem on that particular Pentecost day were Hebrew Jews and Hellenistic Jews and even some Gentile proselytes to Judaism.

Now when these Hebrew Jews had been dispersed by persecution to various foreign lands and cities, they most likely only spoke to the Jews who were there; but the Hellenistic Jews were not so bound by Judaism, especially those Cyrenians and Cyprians who had become believers; and hence, they had no hesitation in speaking to their own countrymen in these places. The gospel therefore began to be preached also to the Gentiles in Antioch, and many believed in the Lord Jesus. The hand of the Lord was present there.

Let us notice that the church in Antioch was not started by an apostle. It began very differently from the way it had begun in Jerusalem. In Jerusalem the apostles had played a leading role; but in Antioch there was no apostle present, there were only those unknown believers. The hand of the Lord was quite evident as those unknown disciples of Jesus preached the gospel of the Lord to their countrymen. It was the work of God, and many came to the Lord.

We notice in Scripture that there are two different ways by which the church can begin. It may begin by the preaching of the apostles or it may simply begin by the witnessing of God's people who are present in a particular place. It is not true that without an apostle a church cannot begin because we find that the church at Antioch was started by unknown believers. They were unknown to the world but they were certainly known to God.

So many came to the Lord that the news soon traveled back to Jerusalem, and when the church in Jerusalem heard about it, they sent Barnabas to visit them. Barnabas went to Antioch; and when he saw the grace of God in them, he exhorted them that with purpose of heart they should abide with the Lord. He was a good man, full of the Holy Spirit and of faith, and many more came to the Lord. Barnabas soon realized that he could not do all the work by himself. It was beyond him; so he went to Tarsus to seek out Saul. Saul had been the persecutor of the believers until he himself turned to the Lord on his way to Damascus. Having become so on fire for the Lord that when he came back to Jerusalem he was too hot, Saul had to be sent away to his home city of Tarsus (Acts 9:26-30). He probably had remained there several years until this moment when Barnabas went to seek him out and brought him to Antioch, where the two of them ministered to the believers. In fact, for a whole year these two met together with the saints there, teaching them the word of God. Moreover, the Bible tells us that the Lord's disciples were first called Christians in Antioch. Now that is a brief history of how the church at Antioch had its beginning.

God Has Lessons to Teach Us through Antioch Church History

I believe that the reason why the history of the churches in those early days is recorded in the Bible is because God has some things to teach us through these churches and their histories in order that we may learn the life of the church through what God did in these various churches. Accordingly, I would like for us to learn what God wants to teach us through the church in Antioch and its history.

A New Move of the Holy Spirit

First, I believe that the foundation of this church represented a new move of the Holy Spirit. On the day of Pentecost the Holy Spirit had made His first move on the earth, and the church in Jerusalem was the result. As has been pointed out, it had had a glorious beginning; nevertheless, we must take note of the fact that the church in Jerusalem was composed mainly of Jews, both Hebrew and Hellenistic, except for some Gentile proselytes to Judaism. Since Jerusalem was the center of Judaism, they were not able to be free from the tradition of the fathers; they were bound quite closely to Judaism. That explains why at the beginning of church history the Roman Empire did not persecute the church because they considered it as being merely another sect of Judaism, which had a well-recognized legal status with the Roman government. At the beginning, therefore, the testimony of the church was not that distinct in Jerusalem. It was too closely identified with Judaism, and hence, the Holy Spirit had to make a new move in order to separate the church from Judaism.

The Holy Spirit therefore began to move in a new way at Antioch, a Gentile city. Although there were indeed Jews there, the church at Antioch was composed mainly of Gentiles. It was not bound by Judaism; and that is the reason people, in observing the church at Antioch, did not know what to call these believers because they were not Jews. The world could not view it as a sect of Judaism; and so the unbelieving world came up with another name for these people of God. Such, then, was the consequence of this new move of the Spirit.

From the book of Acts we learn that the Holy Spirit made a number of different moves, He not being bound by anything. Not only did He make a new move in Antioch, later on He made another new move in Ephesus (Acts 19), and finally He made still another unique move in Rome (Acts 28:14-31). Throughout church history the Holy Spirit is to be found always moving forward, and thus there will be new moves of the Holy Spirit from time to time. Whenever, for example, something of the Spirit begins to be bound by tradition, the Holy Spirit will make a new move because He is seeking for a pure testimony. This is one thing which we as the people of God today need to learn and always remember. Otherwise, we shall be bound by tradition, we thinking that everything which is old is always better. The Holy Spirit, however, is continually looking for that which, though new, is in reality far more ancient than even what is old, inasmuch as His new moves are always a harking back to God the Father's original purpose and concept in eternity past. Such, then, is the first lesson we need to learn from the Antiochian church history; and in view of this, we need to be open to all of God's moves by His Spirit because they are meant to bring His people back closer and closer to His original concept and intent.

Must Purpose in Heart to Abide with the Lord

Let us take note of a second lesson to be learned from the history of this church. Who were these believers in Antioch? What was their spiritual condition? First of all, we find that they turned to the Lord, which of course is the initial requirement for anyone desiring to become a follower of Jesus. Formerly, they had been idol worshipers, but then they turned to the Lord with their whole hearts. They believed in the gospel of Jesus Christ; they accepted Him as their Savior and turned to Him as their Lord. Yet, they not only *turned* to the Lord, they were exhorted by Barnabas to *abide* with the Lord with purpose of heart. To turn to Him is one thing, but that is just the beginning. Turning to the Lord is not the same as abiding with Him. What is the point of turning to the Lord if you do not abide, continue, remain, and grow in Him? If you are not being rooted and grounded in Christ Jesus (cf. Colossians 2:7, Ephesians 3:17), then what is the reason for anyone to have initially turned to Him in the first instance? To continue and grow in the Lord requires the believer to purpose in his/her heart to do so.

Too often God's people today, having by the grace of God been saved, do not purpose in their heart to abide with the Lord. In other words, many are saved but far too many of them do not seek the Lord with their whole heart; and this is why so much weakness currently exists among God's people.

We are reminded, are we not, of the Old Testament prophet Daniel, who when just a teen-ager, had purposed in his heart not to be polluted by the king's food and wine (Daniel 1:4a, 8). Indeed, he would rather live a pure, simple, common life than to be polluted by that which was luxurious, royal, and great in the eyes of men. To have chosen such a way of life took purpose.

Do we have such a purpose in heart? Since we are the Lord's, have we purposed to follow Him all the way? Do we remain in Christ Jesus? God has put us in Christ Jesus, but do we make Him our home? Do we stay there? Or are we merely drifting in and out, having no purpose and not setting our hearts towards the Lord? The Bible says, "My son, give Me your heart, and your eyes will delight in My ways" (see Proverbs 23:26). Oftentimes we who are God's people today do not delight in His ways. We think God's ways are too difficult, too hard, too unreasonable. The reason for this is that we have not given our hearts to the Lord; but if we give our hearts to Him, we will delight in His way and ways. We shall find that His way is perfect, His way is acceptable and good.

Instructed in God's Word

There is a third lesson for us to learn. These believers in Antioch, with purpose of heart, continued to abide with the Lord. They continued to seek and grow in Him; they loved the Lord; and so they persevered. Then for a whole year, they were taught in the word of God. How necessary it is that we be taught in God's word because there is only one way that the church can be built and that is by His word. These believers truly learned the way of the Lord by means of God's word for a whole year. And because of this, the disciples of Christ were first called Christians in Antioch. They were His true disciples.

I remember being impressed by what I had observed among some Christians whom I visited while in India back in 1942. This that I witnessed occurred in the southern Indian city of Madras, and the brothers and sisters there had been meeting for a year by that time. I was told that during that first year of existence as a church they met twice a day every day. Before they went to work, they came together to be taught in the word of God, and after work they came together again to be instructed in God's word. And mind you, this had taken place for an entire year. It so happened that I was there during World War II, and hence there were blackouts in the evenings requiring the people at times to disperse. But when I saw these brethren who had been meeting for only a year—oh, how they loved the Lord and His word! We sometimes think that to meet other than on the Lord's day is just too much. We may perhaps think it is a waste of our time because we have so many other things to do. Nevertheless, one thing is very much needed: to come together to be instructed in God's word.

Believers Are Disciples

A fourth lesson can be learned from the history of the Antiochian church: believers are also disciples. There should be no distinction between these two, but today, unfortunately, we find that believers and disciples are two different categories of persons: a person can be a believer without being a disciple. In those early days back then at Antioch there was no such distinction. If you believed in Jesus, you were discipled to Him. If you received Christ as your Savior, then you accepted Him as your Lord. If you permitted Him to come into your heart, then you automatically allowed Him to rule in your heart. The preponderance of believers in Antioch were Gentiles even as are we; yet, so unlike too many of today's believers, they had turned to the Lord with purpose of heart, had abided with Him, and had been daily taught; and thus, they were true disciples of the Lord Jesus.

Jesus' Disciples
First Called Christians at Antioch

There is a fifth lesson which God's people today can learn from Antioch's disciples. When the world looked at them, they did not know what to call them. They could not call them a sect of the Nazarene—that is to say, a sect of Judaism, because they for the most part were Gentiles. The unbelieving world feels very uncomfortable if they cannot label something or someone foreign to themselves because such uncertainty makes them feel insecure. So when the world of that day observed these people at Antioch and their way of life, they wondered: Who *are* these people? In the end they gave the Antiochian believers the nickname of "Christian." Now let us be very clear here that the label of "Christian" was a nickname which had been given by the *world* and not by the believers themselves. The latter did not call themselves by that name; but, rather, it was the unbelieving world who recognized them as Christians.

Now as you carefully read the book of Acts you will discover that at the beginning Christ's followers were either called "believers" or "disciples" or "the people of the Way" because theirs was a way of life which was so different from all other ways of life on the earth. But, then, at a certain point in the book of Acts we learn that it was those disciples of Jesus in Antioch who were the first to be called "Christians" by the world (11:26).

Why were these particular believers at Antioch called by that name? And what did the world mean to convey by calling them by that name? Well, to the world of unbelievers the name "Christian" simply meant "Christ-man" or "Christ-one." Why, then, did the world call them "Christ-ones"? It is because the people of the world had come across those who were centered upon Christ and upon nothing and no one else: they believed in Christ, they prayed to Christ, they praised Christ, they gathered together in the name of Christ, they sang songs to Christ, they worshiped Christ, they continually mentioned the name of Christ, and they lived totally for Christ. In other words, these were a people who were obsessed with Christ and were fully occupied with Him. Nothing else seemed to matter to them anymore. Nothing was more important to them than Christ Jesus. The world not only heard about Christ *from* them, they saw Christ *in* them. The world of unbelievers recognized them

The Church in Antioch

in that way and hence they could not call these disciples of Christ by any other name than "Christ-ones"—or, Christians.

Today, *we* call ourselves Christians; but when the world looks at *us*, does it see us as true Christians or does it see us as being the same as *it* is, or even worse? How often we hear people of the world say, "Well, now, those so-called Christians are not as good as we are." Let us clearly understand that the term of "Christian" is a name that needs to be *earned*; it is not simply a name by which we conveniently call ourselves. You and I have to earn it from the mouth of the world: Does the world see Christ in our lives or does it see us as being no different from itself?

In the Bible the term Christian is only used three times, the first time here in Acts 11:26. The second instance occurs in Acts 26:28. The timing of it was when Paul was before King Agrippa and Festus the governor. On this occasion he was given the opportunity to defend himself against his Jewish accusers. Instead of defending himself, however, Paul as it were stood up in defense of Christ. In point of fact he preached Christ to all those present. Whereupon Agrippa said, "Paul, in a very little while you will persuade me to be a Christian." To the unbelieving world of that day the word Christian was considered to be a word of derision and contempt. The Governor himself, at a certain point in the proceedings, had interrupted the apostle with this observation: "Paul, you are mad. You have been given a chance to deliver yourself, but you madly insist on preaching Christ instead" (see 26:24). In other words, back then a Christian was deemed to be one who was madly in love with Christ.

The third and final time for the word Christian to be mentioned in Scripture is found in I Peter 4: "If you suffer as a Christian, do not be ashamed, but glorify God under this name" (see v.16). In those early days of the church a Christian was one who was willing to suffer for the name of Christ. Are we in our day willing to suffer for Christ under that name, or are we ashamed of His name?

Thank God, today you would deem it an honor if anyone in the world could say you are a Christian, for in that case you will have earned it. But if people should look at you but could hardly see anything in you which would warrant them calling you a Christian, it would be to your shame.

Interrelationship between Churches

A sixth lesson we can learn from the church in Antioch concerns the interrelationship which existed between churches of that day. When the news came to Jerusalem that many had come to the Lord in Antioch, the brothers and sisters in Jerusalem were very much interested and concerned for their spiritual well-being. Although Jerusalem was in Judea and Antioch was in somewhat distant Syria, and though those believers in Jerusalem were mostly Jews and those in Antioch were mostly Gentiles, nevertheless, when the believers in Jerusalem heard that the Gentiles in Antioch had believed in the Lord, they were interested and they were concerned. So they sent Barnabas to visit them.

Because of what by this time God had done in the house of the Roman centurion Cornelius (Acts 10), the Lord had somehow removed some of the prejudices of the Jewish believers; for they had even been brought to acknowledge that God had in fact also granted to the Gentiles the repentance that leads to life (Acts 11:18). So when the Jerusalem saints heard that the Gentiles in Antioch had believed in the Lord Jesus, it did not come as a total surprise to them. They were therefore somewhat prepared for it, and hence they were concerned for them because they now considered those Gentile believers in Antioch as their brothers and sisters in the Lord and as fellow members in the same body of Christ. So they sent a messenger to visit them.

The Church in Antioch

Whom did the believers in the Jerusalem church send? They sent Barnabas. Now who was this brother? We have already mentioned that he was a Hellenistic Jew, a Levite, but he came from Cyprus. He was thus not a person who was bound by the traditions and teachings of Judaism. Please notice that they did not send an apostle such as Peter or John to Antioch. If they had sent either one of them, it would have given the impression that a brother apostle like them had been sent out to put the church at Antioch under the wings of the church in Jerusalem—meaning that such a sent-one had come to control. No; they sent out a believer who was a Hellenistic Jew, a man with a big heart, who was sympathetic to those Gentiles anywhere who turned to the Lord. Barnabas was not sent out to bring them under the control of the church in Jerusalem as the mother church and thus make the church in Antioch a daughter church—no such thing. He was sent out exclusively for fellowship.

This that has been said is a very important principle in the word of God: every church on earth is independent in government; that is to say, every local assembly of believers is directly responsible to the Lord himself for what occurs therein. There is no such idea in Scripture of a central church headquarters; no such concept of there being a mother church and subordinate daughter churches; no such notion in Scripture of there being some such central church control, no centralization or central government over the local churches. To the contrary, Scripture makes clear that every church is independently dependent itself upon the Lord, and yet all the churches are to be in fellowship with each other in the Spirit.

No church is so independent that it stands by itself: there will be fellowship between churches, but such fellowship will be conducted in the Spirit and not in administration. One church is concerned with the other churches; one church wants to help the other churches; and vice versa. Such is to be the interrelationship that is carried on between and among churches. Not only will there be an interrelationship between individual members of the body of Christ, there will also be fellowship among churches that God by His Spirit has established and is building up on the earth.

So Barnabas went to Antioch to fellowship, to encourage, to exhort and to help—but *not* to control on behalf of Jerusalem. However, fellowship—according to the Scriptures—ought always to be a two-way reality. On the one hand, the church in Jerusalem sent Barnabas to help the church in Antioch to be built up; and on the other hand, the church in Antioch, hearing through the mouth of the prophet Agabus that there was to be a great famine upon the whole earth, sent financial help to the church in Judea. At that time those Gentile believers in Antioch were more well-off than the Jewish believers in Jerusalem. So we witness here that fellowship was a two-way affair back then: the Gentile believers received spiritual help from the Jewish believers, and the Gentile believers responded with love to those Jewish believers who were in need. Such is to be the interrelationship between churches, and a very important principle to observe. The reason Christianity is the way it is today with regard to this Biblical principle is because it has deviated from the word of God.

God's Workmen: Produced in the Church

There is one final lesson which can be learned from the history of the Antiochian believers. In the church in Antioch there eventually came to be raised up in their midst five prophets and teachers (Acts 13:1). Let us be reminded that the church there was not started by an apostle. Even at this later stage in its history there was still no apostle there, but God raised up from among them five prophets and teachers. Those five servants of God ministered His word locally. Thus these believers were not dependent upon an apostle to come from elsewhere and minister to them. Furthermore, it is also true that

The Church in Antioch

everyone in the local church can exhort one another. However, God also chooses to raise up men as prophets and teachers and gives them to the church to minister His word (Ephesians 4:11-12). So we see from this Biblical principle that ministry of God's word in the local church is not one man's ministry, as we find in Christianity today; nor is it all men's ministry, in which anyone and everyone can minister the word of God.

With that as background, let us take note of who these five prophets and teachers were. They included Barnabas and Saul and three others, and all were very different from one another. One was a black man and one had even been raised up in the royal court (see again Acts 13:1). And yet these five ministered together; and as they ministered to the Lord in worship and with prayer and fasting, the Holy Spirit began to speak. But bear in mind that before anyone can minister to man he needs first to minister to the Lord. These men knew how to minister the word of God as prophets and teachers because they first ministered to the Lord, waited upon Him, sought His face, and waited for God to reveal His will to them. So as they ministered to the Lord, they were prepared for what next occurred. The Holy Spirit said, "Separate for Me from these five Barnabas and Saul for the apostolic work to which I have called them" (see 13:2). Hence, instead of a church being started by an apostle, apostles were produced through the church.

How, then, do God's workmen come forth? It is not by people attending a seminary but His servants are raised up in the local church itself: as brothers are together, helping each other, growing together in the Lord, and learning of Him together, at a certain point a church is established and out of it will come forth God's workmen. That is the way God will raise up and train His workmen. Therefore, out of Antioch, not only prophets and teachers but even apostles were produced.

These are some of the lessons which we need to learn from the history of the church in Antioch.

Dear Lord, we want to thank Thee for showing us in Thy word what happened in the church at Antioch. Thou truly hast done great things there, and Thou art doing the same things even today. Lord, we do pray that Thou wilt open our eyes that we may see Thy way with the church, that we may follow Thee. We ask in Thy name. Amen.

Chapter Five

THE CHURCHES IN GALATIA

Acts 13:1-3—Now there were in Antioch, in the [church] which was there, prophets and teachers: Barnabas, and Simeon who was called Niger, and Lucius the Cyrenian, and Manaen, foster-brother of Herod the tetrarch, and Saul. And as they were ministering to the Lord and fasting, the Holy Spirit said, Separate me now Barnabas and Saul for the work to which I have called them. Then, having fasted and prayed, and having laid their hands on them, they let them go.

Acts 13:13-14a—And having sailed from Paphos, Paul and his company came to Perga of Pamphylia; and John separated from them and returned to Jerusalem. But they, passing through from Perga, came to Antioch of Pisidia.

Acts 14:20-23—But while the disciples encircled him, he rose up and entered into the city. And on the morrow he went away with Barnabas to Derbe. And having announced the glad tidings to that city, and having made many disciples, they returned to Lystra, and Iconium, and Antioch, establishing the souls of the disciples, exhorting them to abide in the faith, and that through many tribulations we must enter into the kingdom of God. And having chosen them elders in each [church], having prayed with fastings, they *committed them to the Lord, on whom they had believed.*

Galatians 1:6-12—I wonder that ye thus quickly change, from him that called you in Christ's grace, to a different gospel, which is not another one; but there are some that trouble you, and desire to pervert the glad tidings of the Christ. But if even we or an angel out of heaven announce as glad tidings to you anything besides what we have announced as glad tidings to you, let him be accursed. As we have said before, now also again I say, If any one announce to you as glad tidings anything besides what ye have received, let him be accursed. For do I now seek to satisfy men or God? or do I seek to please men? If I were yet pleasing men, I were not Christ's bondman. But I let you know, brethren, as to the glad tidings which were announced by me, that they are not according to man. For neither did I receive them from man, neither was I taught them, but by revelation of Jesus Christ.

Galatians 6:11-16—See how long a letter I have written to you with my own hand. As many as desire to have a fair appearance in the flesh, these compel you to be circumcised, only that they may not be persecuted because of the cross of Christ. For neither do they that are circumcised themselves keep the law; but they wish you to be circumcised, that they may boast in your flesh. But far be it from me to boast save in the cross of our Lord Jesus Christ, through whom the world is crucified to me, and I to the world. For in Christ Jesus neither is circumcision anything, nor uncircumcision; but new creation. And as many as shall walk by this rule, peace upon them and mercy, and upon the Israel of God.

The Antioch Church's Five Prophets and Teachers

As was mentioned last time, in the church at Antioch there were five prophets and teachers. They were not part of the governing group of elders of the church but they were those whom the Lord had raised up to minister the word of God in that church.

Barnabas

As we consider these five more closely, the first one identified by name, Barnabas, is somewhat familiar to us. That name was actually given to him by the Jerusalem apostles. Formerly he was called Joseph, who was a Levite from Cyprus; but he was renamed Barnabas, meaning, "a son of consolation" because he had such a big and compassionate heart. So Barnabas was the one who was sent forth by the church in Jerusalem to visit those believers in the Gentile cities. As the Scriptures also tell us, he was a man full of faith and of the Holy Spirit. But he was also a man who knew his limitation, for we will remember that he went to Tarsus to seek out Saul and bring him to Antioch that together they might serve the brothers and sisters there. Now that was Barnabas.

Simeon

The second of these five identified was one named Simeon, who was also called Niger, meaning "black." We do not know exactly who this person was, but one thing we do know is that he was a black person, who probably was from Africa.

Lucius

Then there was Lucius, the Cyrenian, from the North African Roman province of Cyrenaica (part of modern-day Libya). Again we are not very sure who that person was. Probably he was among those Cyprians and Cyrenians who had been scattered from Jerusalem because of persecution, and who had ended up at Antioch and who not only preached to the Jews but also to the Gentiles there (see Acts 11:19-20). So probably, Lucius was one of them. Some Bible scholars have even said that he may have been a kinsman of Paul, because in Paul's letter to the Romans the apostle mentioned some of his kinsmen and Lucius' name was among them (16:21). The word kinsmen there simply meant fellow Jews, and hence, this Lucius at Antioch was probably that person. But we really do not know any more about him than this.

Manaen

There was another one called Manaen (the Greek form of the Hebrew name of Menahem), foster-brother of Herod the tetrarch. This Herod was one of the sons of King Herod the Great and who also bore the name of Herod Antipas. This man Manaen had been brought up in company with Herod Antipas, which would indicate that he came from a higher class of Jews.

Saul

Finally, there was Saul the one who would later be known as Paul the apostle. We are familiar with him because formerly he was the Pharisee of Pharisees who had persecuted the church. He was met by the risen and ascended Jesus while on his way to Damascus and was converted and almost immediately thereafter became a servant of the Lord Jesus.

These five men were raised up by God as prophets and teachers in Antioch's local assembly for the purpose of ministering His word to the disciples there. As we have just now seen, all five were very different from each other: their backgrounds were different, where each of them came from was different, their station in life was different. Nevertheless, they all served together as one. The wonderful fact to notice here is that they were ministering to the Lord. We often think that those who minister the word of the Lord only minister to the saints; but let us be clear that before anyone can minister to the saints they need first to minister to the Lord. These five first drew near to the Lord, waited upon Him, worshiped Him, and waited for His word to come upon them before they went before the brethren and ministered to them.

The Apostolic Journey of Paul and Barnabas

Now while these five prophets and teachers were ministering to the Lord with fasting, the Holy Spirit spoke forth: "Set apart for Me Barnabas and Saul for the work that I have called them to do." When the Holy Spirit spoke, those five brothers listened; *and*, they obeyed. The other three of them would probably have liked very much for Barnabas and Saul to remain with them so that they might continue to minister together; yet they all obeyed the Holy Spirit. And after they had fasted and prayed further, the three laid hands on the two and sent them forth. Thus was the beginning of the apostolic work of the apostle Paul. Chapters 13 and 14 of Acts is the record of what happened on this journey for the Lord.

Perga of Pamphylia

Barnabas and Paul (at that time he was still known as Saul but would soon be called by his Christian name) went out together. Quite naturally, the first place they visited was the large island of Cyprus because that had been the homeland of

Barnabas. So they traveled throughout the whole island and then they crossed over the sea to Perga of Pamphylia. It was at this place, incidentally, that their assistant, John Mark, left them and returned home to Jerusalem.

On this first apostolic journey—which probably occurred between the years 47-49 A.D.—these two would spend most of their nearly two-and-a-half-years' time in the southern part of Galatia. Having come to Perga of Pamphylia, Barnabas and Saul, instead of announcing the gospel there, left Perga and went north to Antioch of Pisidia. Why did they do this? According to the New Testament scholar, Sir William Ramsey, it may have been that it was in Pamphylia where Paul had contracted and come down with malaria fever, and because of this, they had to go to higher land. So they went north about a hundred miles to Antioch of Pisidia, which was some 3,600 feet above sea level. So most likely that was the reason they ended up traveling into the Roman province of Galatia where, as was noted earlier, these two apostles would spend most of their time on this first journey of Paul's.

Antioch of Pisidia

Now when these two arrived in Antioch of Pisidia, and as would now be their custom, they went first to the local synagogue on the Sabbath because that was where the Jews and the worshiping Gentiles were gathered together. As will be seen, this was a ready audience. In the synagogues of that day there was much freedom, for after the reading of Scriptures from the Prophets and the Torah, if those in charge noticed someone who looked like a teacher, and even though that one might be a total stranger, they would inquire of that visitor if he had anything to say. And sure enough, on the day of Barnabas and Paul's visit the ruler of the synagogue, upon the Scripture having been read, approached the two apostles and asked: "Strangers, do you have anything to say?" Such was the degree of freedom which then existed in the synagogue. So Paul stood

The Churches in Galatia

up and presented the gospel of Jesus Christ and the grace of God to the people in attendance. He told them how Jesus Christ was the seed of David, how He was crucified and raised from the dead, and how people who were not able to be saved under the law of Moses could now be saved by this Man Jesus Christ.

After Paul delivered his first message in Galatia many of the Jews and some of the worshiping Gentiles followed the two apostles, who then persuaded them to continue in the grace of God. By the next Sabbath the whole city had gathered to hear Paul and Barnabas. Seeing the crowds, the unbelieving Jews in the city became very jealous and began to publicly contradict Paul. So much so that Paul and Barnabas felt it necessary to tell them that the gospel of Jesus Christ must first be presented to the Jews because they were the chosen people of God, having been prepared by God for the coming of the Messiah; but if they now rejected Him, then, declared Paul and Barnabas, "we must go to the Gentiles because the Messiah is the light for the nations as well." When the Gentiles present heard *those* words of Paul, they were very happy because they saw that the door to salvation was also opened to them, and hence, many came to the Lord. So Paul and Barnabas separated themselves from the synagogue, and continued to stay in Pisidian Antioch for a while longer. Moreover, the word of grace spread all over the region round about.

But the unbelieving Jews were so jealous that they incited the leading citizens of the city. Whereupon the local authorities cast the two apostles out of Antioch of Pisidia. Yet, though they were driven out of the city, the disciples who remained behind were filled with joy and with the Holy Spirit. Now we would think that when these two men were cast out and the disciples were left as sheep without a shepherd, they would probably be filled with sorrow and sadness and say among themselves, "What shall we do now? Our teachers are gone." Instead, they were full of joy and the Holy Spirit (13:52). That was the beginning of the church in Antioch of Pisidia.

Iconium

After Paul and Barnabas were expelled they went southeast about ninety miles to Iconium, which was a metropolitan city of the Lycaonian district. As usual, on the Sabbath they again entered the synagogue and presented the gospel of Jesus Christ to the people present. Many of the Jews and Gentiles believed in the Lord Jesus, but again, it stirred up the jealousy of the unrepentant Jews, so there was opposition once more. However, in spite of the opposition the apostles stayed there for a long while, announcing the glad tidings of the Lord Jesus with boldness, and the Holy Spirit bore witness to their preaching with signs and wonders. Eventually the whole city was divided because whenever the gospel is preached, it divides people into the believing and the nonbelieving. There was even a plot set afoot to stone the apostles. But when the two of them heard about it, they fled from Iconium and went farther southeast some forty miles away and into another place called Lystra.

Lystra

Evidently there was no synagogue in Lystra, for it was a grossly heathen city. So instead of going to any synagogue Barnabas and Paul conducted open-air meetings. It so happened that there was a man present who was born lame and had never walked; but when he listened to the gospel of Jesus Christ, Paul discerned that there was faith in him; so he called out: "Rise up and walk!" The lame man stood up and walked. Because of this miracle, and since Lystra was a heathen city, the crowds thought the gods had appeared. They called Barnabas "Jupiter" but Paul they called "Mercury" because he was the one who spoke the most. From the temple of Jupiter just outside the city its priest began to bring bulls garlanded with flowers in order to offer sacrifices to the apostles. This was the subtlety of the Enemy.

In the two previous cities there was opposition and persecution, but here God's servants were welcomed and honored as gods. But thank God, Paul and Barnabas saw through the subtlety of the Enemy. They rushed into the midst of the crowd, tore their clothes, and stopped them, saying, "We are but men like you; it is God who is calling people to repentance." They were barely able to stop the people from performing such foolish acts.

But then we see how changeable the people at Lystra could be, for when the unbelieving Jews coming from Pisidian Antioch and Iconium stirred up this same people who had earlier wanted to honor Barnabas and Paul as gods, they turned against them and stoned Paul nearly to death. In fact, we do not know whether he was truly dead or not, but the people thought he was dead. So they literally dragged him out of the city and left him there; but the newly-believing disciples lovingly gathered around him. And, then, suddenly Paul stood up and walked back into the city. Whether he had died or not, it was truly a miracle. The very next day the two apostles left Lystra and went farther southeast to a nearby adjoining city called Derbe.

Derbe

At that time Derbe was a Roman frontier city within this same province of Galatia. It was a small town and Paul and Barnabas remained there for some little while. It seemed as though everything here was quiet; there was no opposition. Many came to the Lord through their gospel preaching and so additional disciples were made. That was the geographical extent of Paul's first apostolic trip out from Syrian Antioch.

The Return Journey

Now after their time at Derbe the apostles made a return journey from there back to Lystra, Iconium and Pisidian Antioch. In this first trip of Paul's outbound the apostles' ministry was preaching the gospel of Jesus Christ and the grace of God, the result of which many came to the Lord. But in their journey back from Derbe their work was that of strengthening the souls of the disciples, exhorting them to abide in the faith, and helping them to see that all must suffer much tribulation in order to enter the kingdom of God. So it was more a work of establishing them in the Lord. Also, they appointed elders for them in each church and committed them to the Lord. Thus came to an end this first apostolic journey of Paul and Barnabas who had been sent out by the Holy Spirit.

The Churches of Galatia Born

Let us notice that Paul, when writing his Letter to the Galatians, opened it with greetings addressed to the "churches of Galatia" (1:2). Why did the apostle write in that manner? It is because Galatia was not a city but a Roman province which was composed of many cities, in each of which God had raised up a testimony to His name. Accordingly, the various churches of Galatia were never referred to as "the church of Galatia" but always referred to as "the churches of Galatia." Moreover, these churches were never a federation; which is to say that they were never joined together organizationally. Instead, because all these individual local churches were in the same province and were thus in close proximity to each other, therefore, they had very close fellowship one with another. So when Paul wrote his letter, he addressed it as to the churches in Galatia.

The Preaching and Travail of the Apostles

Each of these churches came into being as a result of two things which occurred in each locality. First, through the preaching of the gospel of Jesus Christ and the Holy Spirit touching the hearts of those who heard the gospel the people in each community repented and believed in the Lord Jesus. And hence, these believers became the members of the body of Christ in that particular locality. But second, these churches also came into being through the travail of the apostles. How the apostles suffered because of their preaching the gospel among the inhabitants in each of the localities; nevertheless, through the tribulation and affliction which Paul and Barnabas experienced, these two servants of God were able to bring many people to Jesus and gather them to the Lord. So all these churches came into being through the preaching of the gospel and also through the travail of the apostles.

All these churches, except probably the one at Derbe, were born in tribulation because almost always wherever the gospel was preached back then, it was so much different from the world that the world would rise up and try to destroy it. Therefore, since these churches were born in tribulation, their separation from the world was naturally very complete. In one sense that is a good thing, because if a church begins in peace without any suffering or any opposition from the world, the brothers and sisters there will most likely not be so separated from the world. Indeed, that is the problem we find in churches today. But thank God, in those early days when the gospel was preached there was always separation, as in fact there should be, because the gospel preached back then always raised up the opposition of the world.

The Establishing of Elders

The apostles preached the gospel to them and remained with them for a while, but they never organized them into churches. They left them to the Lord and to the Holy Spirit, and off they went to another place. But when they returned to these churches after a year or two, they noticed that the brothers and sisters had grown in the Lord, and that the Holy Spirit had already manifested those who should be elders. The apostles recognized the fact and appointed them as elders (Acts 14:23). From all this we can discern that a church is never organized; it is born. Even though there will be some organization necessary, like elders being appointed, what is evident is that in those various local churches there is the manifestation of life. It was not something done by man nor was it something mechanical or something technical. It was something that grew out of life. Whenever life begins to grow, an order will come into being. And that was what we find in the churches of Galatia.

Paul's Letter to the Churches of Galatia

These churches in Galatia were the first love of the apostle Paul because they were the results of his first labor, and usually, one's first labor will be one's first love. He loved these brethren, but after ten years had gone by, which would have been around 57 A.D., we find that the apostle found it necessary to write a letter to the churches of Galatia. And it was a letter of deep anguish and of profound sorrow. Why was this so? For had not these churches of Galatia possessed a wonderful beginning and had not their relationship with the apostle Paul been quite dear and most precious? This was manifestly true, for in his letter to them Paul mentioned that when he had first come into their midst he had been in great weakness due to his having most likely contracted malaria fever that can sometimes cause a person to shake; and also his eyesight had been affected. And yet the brethren in these churches had loved him so much that if possible they would have been willing to have had their own eyes removed and given to the apostle Paul (Galatians 4:13-15). Such was the close, loving relationship which had existed between Paul and the churches of Galatia. So why now did this apostle need to write a letter to them that was full of great anguish and sorrow?

Believers Who Return to the Law

Paul had to write such a letter to them ten years later because during those intervening years some Judaizers—who actually had believed in Jesus themselves—had entered into the

Galatian disciples' midst and had persuaded them on this wise: "You believe in the Lord Jesus, but if you want to be perfect, you have to keep the law. You must be circumcised, you have to keep days and festivals; and by so doing, that will complete and perfect you" (Galatians 4:5-11). Those Galatian brothers and sisters, in their ignorance and probably in their desire to become fully spiritual quickly (do we not all want to be spiritual quickly also?), had unfortunately hearkened to the teaching of these Judaizers. What had happened was that with the passing of a number of years since Paul and Barnabas had been with them, and as they moved on with the Lord, these Galatian brethren found that their progress in the Lord was progressing very slowly; yet they had greatly desired to be perfected and to do so in as short a time as possible.

Unexpectedly, some outsiders came among them with enticing words, saying: "Yes, there is indeed a way to be perfected but you cannot become so by merely believing in the Lord Jesus. If you truly want to become perfect, and quickly, you have to keep the law: you must be circumcised and you will be instantly perfected" (Galatians 5:11-12, 6:12-13). That kind of teaching quite naturally appealed to their flesh for the flesh always wants to do something. If someone tells you that the flesh can do nothing, such teaching is very humiliating and degrading. Man's flesh always likes to do and accomplish something so that he may have that of which to boast. In coming to the Lord Jesus a person has nothing of which to boast because there is no righteousness of his own. But the essence of the gospel is that human beings must come to Jesus as sinners and accept the grace of God completely, there being nothing we can do but believe on Jesus Christ. We must depend completely on the grace of the Lord Jesus. To do so, however, is very humiliating and that is why many proud people never come to the Lord.

I am reminded of the story of the American evangelist Charles Finney, who had been a lawyer in his earlier years; and while studying the law, he discovered that the American legal system sometimes referred to the Bible. So he obtained a Bible as a book of reference and began to read it. And at a certain point, the Spirit of God had seriously begun to convict him. He therefore began to read the Bible more, and not just as a reference volume. But whenever he saw somebody entering his office, he quickly hid his Bible. One day while in the process of going to his office, the burden of his soul was so heavy upon him that instead of going any farther to the office, Finney went to some woods nearby. He walked quite far into the woods because he did not want anybody to see him. He found a place with a fallen tree, so he knelt down and began to pray. But before he did so he uttered a kind of vow: "Either I die or I get saved. Otherwise, I will never come out of these woods." Then he began to pray. Finney thought he could easily set himself to pray in those woods, but whenever he heard some rustling sound in the forest he instantly got up and looked around because he did not want anybody to see him kneeling there and praying. This phenomenon happened a few times that day; and hence, greatly frustrated, he was now quite sorry he had made such a vow. Unable to pray anymore, Finney wondered to himself what he should do. At that very moment the Holy Spirit convicted him of his pride: "You are a sinner seeking forgiveness, and yet you are afraid people might see you kneeling here and asking for forgiveness. What a proud man you are!" Instantly pricked in heart, Finney repented of his pride and was wonderfully saved.

We are naturally very proud; we want to do something. Even after we are saved we still want to do something. Is that not true? It is as Paul wrote in his Letter to the Galatians: "You began with the Spirit of grace, but you are now trying to be completed and perfected with the flesh" (see 3:3). I believe each one of us has either done that or is still doing that. We believe in the Lord Jesus according to His grace; but very soon we begin to move into the area of the law by moving back into our flesh.

We begin to try to do something ourselves in order to be matured and perfected spiritually. Perhaps we may even say to ourselves: "To be justified, I have to depend upon the Lord; but to be holy, I must depend on myself." Hence, we try to be holy; we try to be a good Christian; we try to overcome sin; we try to please the Lord; in short, we try to do everything ourselves. The heart may be right, yet how subtle is the Enemy: for we are unaware of his moving us away from Christ into ourselves, away from grace into law, away from the Holy Spirit and back to the flesh (cf. Galatians 5:2-6).

Those believers in Galatia had been cleverly enticed by the Judaizers (Galatians 1:7b). They had returned to the law so that they would have something of which to boast in their flesh (cf. Galatians 6:12-15). They did not discern the subtlety of the Enemy. But thank God for Paul. He saw through the Enemy's tactic and realized that this was not a small matter but was that which perverted the truth of the gospel of Jesus Christ at its very core (again, 1:7b).

The Gospel of Grace

What is the gospel of Jesus Christ? It is the gospel of grace, the gospel of faith, the gospel of the Holy Spirit. In other words, the self—the flesh—is crucified on the cross because there is no good in the flesh and, therefore, you cannot depend upon the flesh in any way. In short, if you try to do anything on your own without the Holy Spirit, you are being enticed away from Christ.

So when Paul heard about these things, it hurt him so deeply that he wrote a letter to the Galatian believers. Usually, because of his impaired eyesight, Paul would dictate the letter's text, someone would set it down on parchment, and finally he would sign his name to the letter. This letter, however, he wrote down on the parchment himself. "What a long letter I have written," he noted—which for the unhealthy apostle *was* long since he wrote it out himself because he was so disturbed and so in anguish over the spiritual situation among these Galatian brethren.

Paul loved these disciples very much and wanted to deliver them from the Enemy of their souls, so he employed very strong language in his letter. Wrote Paul: "The gospel which you supposedly have received is *not* the gospel. There is only one gospel—that of Jesus Christ: He is everything. From the beginning to the very end, He is the door, the way, the beginning, and the perfection. Everything is in Christ Jesus; and if that be true, and it most surely is, then you cannot employ any means to salvation and Christian perfection outside of Him. All is dependent upon Christ and God's grace. And that is what a Christian is, that is what the church is, and that is what the gospel is. Whatever is outside of Christ leads us away from Christ—the law, works, the flesh. All such is but "another gospel." Interestingly enough, the meaning of the word another which Paul used here is that *that* gospel is another of a *different* kind. The apostle went on to say that "whoever preaches that kind of gospel, whether even I or an angel from heaven, let him be accursed."

Now that was extremely strong language for him to have used. In so many words Paul was saying here that if he were to come back to them and preach another gospel—in this case, mixing law with grace—he was to be accursed; even an angel was to be accursed were he to do the same thing. Today we find that among some so-called groups of Christianity there are people who supposedly hear the voice of the angels give a message, but that message is very different from what the word of God teaches. There is only one gospel and it is Jesus Christ alone. He is the beginning and He is the end: Jesus is all; He is everything.

The Subtlety of the Enemy

The apostle Paul indeed wrote a very strong letter to the churches of Galatia, telling them that the gospel he had preached to them he had not received from man but it had come to him by revelation of Jesus Christ. He mentioned how subtle the Enemy had been in that even Peter, when on one occasion he had visited Syrian Antioch, was led astray. While with the brethren there Peter had been consistently eating with the brothers and sisters who were Gentiles; but when some brothers came from James in Jerusalem, Peter got frightened and separated himself from the Gentile brethren. The rest of the Jews there had also done the same, and even Barnabas was affected. So Paul, even though he was younger, confronted Peter publicly before everyone in the church and withstood him to the face, pointing out his error (Galatians 2:11-16). And thank God for Peter that he humbly accepted a younger brother's convicting word; for we find in Peter's second epistle an acknowledgement that "our beloved brother Paul" has stated in his writings "some things hard to be understood," but they are nonetheless part of God's word (3:15-16).

It is Paul's Letter to the Galatians which revealed for us how the entire spiritual condition among the Galatian churches had greatly changed for the worse over the intervening decade of years since he and Barnabas had first preached the true gospel to the people of that Roman province. We do not know what the result of that letter was. We hope it came to them as an eye opener, that they too saw through the subtlety of the Enemy and were mercifully delivered out of his clutches just in time and in due course had returned to Christ Jesus and the gospel of God's grace.

Lessons to Be Learned from the Churches of Galatia

Be Vigilant

What are the lessons we can learn from these churches of Galatia? First, we must recognize that a good beginning does not necessarily guarantee a happy ending. This observation is not only true and relevant to the individual Christian but is also true to the entire church corporately. We all may begin right, but it is the ending that is important. The churches in Galatia began gloriously, but the ending was shameful. So we must never give up. Watch; be vigilant; never be too sure; let us never have any confidence in ourselves. The perseverance of the saints is not brought about by the saints themselves; rather, they are kept by the grace of God. We are what we are by His grace. If we move away from grace and begin to trust in our flesh, we will fall from grace because we are not able to preserve ourselves (cf. Galatians 5:4). It is God who is able to keep us to the very end. How we need to commit ourselves to Him for Him to keep us. It is even as the apostle Paul once declared: "I know whom I have believed and I am fully persuaded that He is able to keep that which I have committed to Him" (see II Timothy 1:12c).

You know whom you have believed, but have you committed yourself to the God of grace? That is the only way by which you can be kept. If you have not committed yourself to Him, given yourself completely to Him, placed yourself in His hands by allowing Him to take care of you, then there is no assurance that you will be able to be kept to the very end. It is the grace of God only that can keep us. So we need to make a commitment.

Many brothers and sisters believe in the Lord, but there is no commitment. They still want to be their own master. They still want to take themselves into their own hands and run their own lives. If you do that, there is great danger lurking there. We need to be a people fully committed to God and His grace because He is the only One who is able to keep us to the very end. Hence, first of all, the lesson to be learned is: Be vigilant once you begin committing yourself to God.

The apostle Paul wrote in I Corinthians: "Be vigilant; stand fast in the faith; quit yourselves like men; be strong" (16:13). And the apostle Peter counseled his readers along the same line: "Be vigilant, watch. Your adversary the devil as a roaring lion walks about seeking whom he may devour. Whom resist, stedfast in faith, knowing that the selfsame sufferings are accomplished in your brotherhood which is in the world" (I Peter 5:8-9).

So the exhortation to us from the life and history of the Galatian churches and the first lesson we need to learn is to never be too sure of ourselves. Our confidence is in God and Him alone. Let us be vigilant, watchful, standing fast in faith and quitting or conducting ourselves like men, being ever strong; because the enemy is like a roaring lion walking throughout the whole world seeking out whomever he can devour (I Peter 5:8).

Never Mix Law with Grace

The second lesson to learn from what happened among the Galatian brethren is for us never to mix law with grace. For doing so changes the very nature of the gospel of Jesus Christ. This was not only true among some first-century believers, it is even more true among believers in our own day. There are quite a number of brethren in Christ who in their teaching and practice are mixing law with grace. Moreover, there are those who, though they may not officially and/or publicly mix law with grace, are nonetheless unconsciously doing so.

How do we know that this work we are undertaking is law and not of grace? How do we know it is not our work? I think the easiest way to discern the difference is: Are we doing it ourselves or are we doing it by the power of the Holy Spirit? If we do something by ourselves, we are keeping the law, it is being done according to a regulation, a rule, a creed, a method. And so it becomes legalistic because *we* are doing the work; but if we realize that without Him we can do nothing (John 15:5), and that it is only by Him that we are able to do it (Philippians 4:13, I Corinthians 15:10), such, it can safely be said, is the work of faith. It is not just a work but it is a work of *faith*; and the work of faith is that which is done by the life and power of the Holy Spirit within us.

Now, outwardly, you may not be able to detect the difference. Here you are doing something; but the source is different, and the result will be different. If you are doing a work by yourself, the result will end up being a boasting in the flesh. If, however, you are doing a work by the life of Christ in you, the result will be that God is glorified. So we need to be very careful about this matter.

Law, works, and flesh always join hands together, just like grace, faith, and the Holy Spirit are joined together. Hence, let us never try to mix up law with grace. We need always to remember that our whole life is a life of grace. We depend upon God and Him alone.

Avoid Whatever Or Whoever Leads Us Away from Christ

The third lesson is that anything or anyone that leads us away from Christ needs to be avoided. Those Judaizers who had come in among the Galatian brethren had themselves believed in the Lord Jesus; but they were adamant in holding to the belief that, in their words, "Christ is not sufficient. Yes, you have to have Christ; but you must have Him plus something else; it must be Christ plus a keeping of the Mosaic law; then you will become perfect." Furthermore, these Judaizers also tried to draw believers away from Paul to themselves (Galatians 4:17).

In view of all this, it is necessary for us to be very, very careful of anyone or anything that could draw us away from Christ and into something else or towards someone else. The danger is there because we know that only Christ is all and in all. This is the will of God—the all-sufficiency of Christ. It is not Christ plus *something* else, nor is it Christ plus *someone* else; it is Christ and Him alone. And that is the gospel truth in its essence. May the Lord keep us.

> *Dear heavenly Father, we do want to thank Thee for giving us these examples from the churches of Galatia and thank Thee for giving us the Letter to the Galatians. Father, we do pray that these examples and these words will truly help us and deliver us from the danger to which we are all exposed. Oh, dear Lord, we pray that Thou wilt search our hearts, that we will not—by any means, by any way, by any people—be drawn away from Thyself. Lord, we pray that we may maintain such a living relationship with Thyself that we see nothing but Jesus only. Oh, do keep us; and do keep the truth of the gospel in the midst of Thy people. We ask in Thy precious name. Amen.*

Chapter Six

THE CHURCH IN PHILIPPI

Acts 16:6-40—And having passed through Phrygia and the Galatian country, having been forbidden by the Holy Spirit to speak the word in Asia, having come down to Mysia, they attempted to go to Bithynia, and the Spirit of Jesus did not allow them; and having passed by Mysia they descended to Troas. And a vision appeared to Paul in the night: There was a certain Macedonian man, standing and beseeching him, and saying, Pass over into Macedonia and help us. And when he had seen the vision, immediately we sought to go forth to Macedonia, concluding that the Lord had called us to announce to them the glad tidings. Having sailed therefore away from Troas, we went in a straight course to Samothracia, and on the morrow to Neapolis, and thence to Philippi, which is the first city of that part of Macedonia, a colony.

And we were staying in that city certain days. And on the sabbath day we went outside the gate by the river, where it was the custom for prayer to be, and we sat down and spoke to the women who had assembled. And a certain woman, by name Lydia, a seller of purple, of the city of Thyatira, who worshipped God, heard; whose heart the Lord opened to attend to the things spoken by Paul. And when she had been baptised and her house, she besought us, saying, If ye have judged me to be faithful to the Lord, come into my house and abide there. And she constrained us. And it came to pass as we were going to prayer that a certain female slave, having a spirit of Python, met us, who brought much profit to her masters by prophesying. She, having followed Paul and us, cried saying, These men are bondmen of the Most High God, who announce to you the way of salvation. And this she did many days. And Paul, being distressed, turned, and said to the spirit, I enjoin thee in the name of Jesus Christ to come out of her. And it came out the same hour. And her masters, seeing that the hope of their gains was gone, having seized Paul and Silas, dragged them into the market before the magistrates; and having brought them up to the praetors, said, These men utterly trouble our city, being Jews, and announce customs which it is not lawful for us to receive nor practise, being Romans. And the crowd rose up too against them; and the praetors, having torn off their clothes, commanded to scourge them. And having laid many stripes upon them they cast them into prison, charging the jailor to keep them safely; who, having received such a charge, cast them into the inner prison, and secured their feet to the stocks. And at midnight Paul and Silas, in praying, were praising God with singing, and the prisoners listened to them. And suddenly there was a great earthquake, so that the foundations of the prison shook, and all the doors were immediately opened, and the bonds of all loosed. And the jailor being awakened out of his sleep, and seeing the doors of the prison opened, having drawn a sword was going to kill himself, thinking the prisoners had fled. But Paul called out with a loud voice, saying, Do *thyself no harm, for we are all here. And having asked for lights, he rushed in, and, trembling, fell down before Paul and Silas. And leading them out said, Sirs, what must I do that I may be saved? And they said, Believe on the Lord Jesus and thou shalt be saved, thou and thy house. And they spoke to him the word of the Lord, with all that were in his house. And he took them the same hour of the night and washed them from their stripes; and was baptised, he and all his straightway. And having brought them into his house he laid the table for them, and rejoiced with all his house, having believed in God. And when it was day, the praetors sent the lictors, saying, Let those men go. And the jailor reported these words to Paul: The praetors have sent that ye may be let go. Now therefore go out and depart in peace. But Paul said to them, Having beaten us publicly uncondemned, us who are Romans, they have cast us into prison, and now they thrust us out secretly? no, indeed, but let them come themselves and bring us out. And the lictors reported these words to the praetors. And they were afraid when they heard they were Romans. And they came and besought them, and having brought them out, asked them to go out of the city. And having gone out of the prison, they came to Lydia; and having seen the brethren, they exhorted them and went away.*

In the book of Acts we see the life of the body of Christ, which is the church. Our emphasis in these messages is on our seeing the life of the church of God in those early days of its history. It began in Jerusalem and continued on to Antioch and to the churches in Galatia. Today let us continue on together to see the life of the church as occurred in Philippi.

This visit to that city was part of the second missionary journey of the apostle Paul. He started out from Syrian Antioch with Silas in the year 50 A.D. and lasted till 53 A.D. In passing through Derbe they picked up Timothy. After they passed through Phrygia and the Galatian areas they traveled west, thinking they would preach the word of God in the large Roman province of Asia (in what is today western Turkey) because it was heavily populated. But the Holy Spirit did not allow them to go there. They therefore continued going farther west to Mysia with the thought of going a little distance north to Bithynia to preach the word of God there, and again the Spirit of Jesus forbade them. The only thing they could do was to go to the most western point, which brought them to Troas, a port along the coast of the Aegean Sea. They literally had nowhere else to go, but upon retiring for the night in Troas, Paul saw in a vision a Macedonian who besought him to come over and help them there. And the Lukan narrative reads: "*We* concluded that it was the Holy Spirit's desire for us to go forth to Macedonia."

Guided by the Holy Spirit

Now we know that the gospel began in Asia. From Jerusalem it was carried to Antioch and from thence to the Galatian areas. But then for the first time the gospel was to be taken and preached in Europe, for Macedonia was located in southeastern Europe, it being part of what is known as Greece. We cannot help but notice that the footsteps of the Lord's servants here were guided by the Holy Spirit. That is the first of several lessons to be learned from considering the founding of the Philippian church. It is the Lord who sets apart His servants, and it is the Spirit of the Lord who decides where they are to go.

Oftentimes we are guided by needs; and in one sense, that is not altogether wrong. Paul and his companions saw the need for the gospel to be announced in the western Roman province of Asia, so they were considering going there. So they laid their thought at the feet of the Lord, but the Holy Spirit did not allow them to go there. Likewise, they saw the need in Bithynia, but instead of going there governed by the need of the gospel, they again laid the matter before the Lord, and the Spirit of Jesus once more forbade them to go to that place. Hence, we can learn from all this that the footsteps of God's servants should be ordered and governed by the Holy Spirit. It is the Holy Spirit who directs them where they should go and what they should do.

Today we find that need oftentimes determines the direction and action of the servants of God. Frequently in our day it is *human* strategy which decides where to go; but here with Paul and his companions it was not needs. The needs are indeed everywhere, but God knows better than all of us, because for Him there is a timing. Yes, the gospel should in fact be preached in the province of Asia; and in his third missionary journey Paul actually focused his gospel efforts on that very area; but let us realize that God has His own timetable: He knows exactly when His word should be preached at a certain place, and that will be *His* strategy, not man's. So we cannot depend upon human strategy. We must learn to inwardly recognize the timing of the Lord; that is to say, we must learn to obey the guidance and the leading of the Holy Spirit.

Here we find that Paul and his companions were quite sensitive in their spirits to the Holy Spirit's guidance. When they were forbidden by Him, they did not go. They simply went on until they had nowhere to go but to the sea; and it was at that moment—indeed, at the right divine moment—that Paul beheld in a vision a Macedonian, and thus the calling of God came to them. So this is the first lesson that we can learn from considering the ministry of Paul and his party in relation to the church at Philippi. So far as the footsteps of God's servants are concerned, they should be guided by the Holy Spirit and not only by human needs.

It was Sir William Ramsey who concluded from his Biblical research that Luke probably was a native of Philippi. Luke's words in Acts 16:10 read: "We concluded to go to Macedonia." The *we* section in the book of Acts begins there, and it breaks off at the end of chapter 16 and is not resumed until Acts 20:5, at which point Luke is recorded as joined once again to Paul in Philippi. Evidently, Luke had been in Troas at the time of Paul's vision and we do not know whether in his vision the Macedonian whom he saw was Luke or somebody else. Nevertheless, God revealed at the right moment where they should go. So Paul and his party crossed the Aegean Sea, some 125 miles distant, and landed at Neapolis, a seaport in Macedonia located only eight to ten miles from Philippi, the first major Macedonian city. From Neapolis they walked to the city of Philippi.

Philippi was a Roman colony. What was a colony? At that time Rome had a great empire; and one way by which the Roman authorities tried to rule the Empire was to set up colonies in different parts of Rome's territories. These colonies were inhabited in part by retired Roman soldiers and their families. Rome cleverly placed these people in certain locations throughout the Empire and made this or that colony a recognized *Roman* city. In a given colony, for instance, everything was Roman in character: the law was Roman; the government was Roman; and the clothing, the way, and the manner of life and customs were according to Rome. And Philippi was one such colony and was therefore an important place.

The inhabitants of Philippi were mostly native Macedonians, along with the retired Roman soldiers and their families, and a number of Orientals from Asia and other places; but there were very few Jews. That was very strange since Philippi actually was located along the route from the East to the West, so it was truly an important city. But inasmuch as there were so few Jews, there was no synagogue there. Now it was generally true that if there were ten Jewish men of leisure residing in a community, there could be a synagogue established. The descriptive phrase "men of leisure" did not mean that such men did nothing; rather, it meant that they were able to set aside some time for Judaism and for worship. Even so, in Philippi there were not even ten Jewish men of leisure, and hence, there was no synagogue; instead, there were only some women who gathered together to worship God outside of the city at a place by the riverside.

The Beginning of the Church in Philippi

Lydia

On their first Sabbath day, which was a few days following their arrival in Philippi, Paul and his companions went out of the city to the riverside and sat down and talked with the women who had gathered there. These women were mostly Jews, but there were also some who worshiped God as Gentile proselytes. Paul spoke to them, announcing the gospel of Jesus Christ. There was one woman by the name of Lydia who, being from the city of Thyatira, was obviously not a European but an Asiatic, since that city was one of the Roman communities in the province of Asia and was one of the seven churches in Asia mentioned in the book of Revelation. Lydia was a seller of purple fabrics, which at that time was the chosen dress material of the wealthy noble people. So she must have been a business woman dealing in rich people's clothing.

Even so, she worshiped God, and while by the river on this Sabbath day listening to Paul, the Lord opened her heart. Lydia believed the gospel that was preached on that day as well as every member in her household. Not only did they believe in the Lord Jesus but they also were baptized. Lydia then besought Paul and his companions, saying that if they truly considered her as being faithful to the Lord, they should come and stay in her house. By this we can assume that it must have been a large house. She having constrained them to do so, Paul and his companions most likely dwelt among Lydia's household while they were in Philippi instead of staying in an inn. They then went about preaching the gospel.

The Slave Girl

While Paul and his co-workers in the gospel were doing that, however, there was a woman who followed them wherever they went. But this woman happened to be a slave having a spirit of Python—that is to say, a spirit of divination. Therefore being demon-possessed, she could tell fortunes and prophesy and thus gain for her masters much profit. While following Paul and his companions she kept crying aloud: "These men are bondmen of the Most High God, who preach to you the gospel of salvation." Is that not strange? Here was a woman possessed by an evil spirit, and yet she was conducting herself as though helping Paul to preach the gospel. Actually, however, it was but another strategy of the devil in his attempt to confuse the issue. Sometimes the devil tries to persecute; but at other times he tries to confuse. After a few days of this, Paul became exasperated. He turned around and said to the evil spirit, "In the name of the Lord Jesus Christ I order you to come out of her"; and the spirit at once came out.

Now because of this, she could no longer prophesy; so her masters saw that their means of profit-making was finished. Immediately they laid hold of Paul and Silas, brought them to the city's magistrates, and said to them: "These Jews have come here to teach us customs that we as Romans cannot receive and practice. Moreover, they are troubling the entire city." The whole city rose up in support of these false accusers. Finally, the magistrates, without attempting to find out the real issues involved, tore off the clothes of Paul and Silas and beat them severely. Paul and Silas were then put into prison, with the jailer having been told to keep them safe. So the jailer placed them in the inner prison—the dungeon—and put their feet in stocks.

The Roman Jailer

Midnight is usually the worst time if you have been physically wounded. You feel the hurt more at midnight. But on this occasion Paul and Silas, having been beaten with many stripes and having most likely bled a lot and feeling great pain, were nonetheless at midnight praying and praising the Lord with singing. What an expression of victory! While they were praising God with singing, all the prisoners were listening, and then there was a great earthquake that shook the prison's very foundation. All the doors of the prison were thus opened and all the prisoners' chains were loosened. The jailer suddenly woke up from his sleep and, seeing the doors were opened, he instantly thought that all the prisoners must have escaped. So he took a sword and was about to kill himself, but Paul called forth from the dungeon and said, "We are all here; therefore, don't harm yourself." Nobody had escaped. The jailer, asking for lights, went inside and, trembling, led Paul and Silas out. He then asked them a question: "What must I do to be saved?" And they told him: "Believe on the Lord Jesus and you shall be saved, both you and your household." Thus did these servants of God speak forth the word of the Lord to him and to all who were in his household; with the result that the jailer took them out of prison, washed their wounds, and set a table of food before them. Also, he and his household were all immediately baptized, with him and his family rejoicing in the Lord.

The next day the magistrates sent messengers, who said to the jailer, "Let those two men go." But Paul said, "We are Roman citizens." And as Roman citizens they could not be lashed and imprisoned without first having been given an opportunity to defend themselves. Paul said, "We are Romans and you scourged us. You put us into prison and now you secretly want to drive us out of the city. No; you magistrates must come and do so yourselves." I believe the reason Paul most likely did this was for the sake of the church brethren who would be left behind. And that was how the gospel came to Philippi.

Worldly Distinctions: Eliminated in the Church

The stay of Paul in Philippi was not too long because, as we have seen, he was ordered to leave the city. Let us pause here for a few moments and take notice of a number of aspects relative to the Philippian church and its founding. First, from the very beginning the church in Philippi was composed of people of different races, cultures, backgrounds, and social status. For example, Lydia was an Asiatic, the slave girl most likely was a Greek, and the jailer was a Roman official: again, Lydia was a rich merchant woman, the slave girl was a social chattel possessing the lowest social status, and of course, the jailer was a Roman officer: and hence, we find that in this Roman colony there were different cultures, different races, and differences in social status among this city's inhabitants. Even so, when the gospel made its appearance in Philippi, all the world's distinctions were eliminated in the church that came into being there: no Jew and no Gentile, no circumcision nor uncircumcision, no bondman or freeman, and neither Barbarian nor Scythian any longer exist when it comes to the church of Jesus Christ (Colossians 3:11); for in the church all these worldly distinctions are eliminated by the gospel, whereas outside the church all these distinctions—race, culture, social status, and so on—continue to exist in the world. And because of that, people of the world are divided. But all who are in Christ are one because when we step through the door that is Christ, the cross has eliminated all such worldly distinctions. As a consequence, in the church there is no such distinction as Asian or European or Greek or Roman; in the church there is to be no such class division between the wealthy or the poor; in the church there are no cultural differences which separate people.

All these are eliminated by the cross of Jesus Christ. In Him we are one, and that is precisely what the church is. And here in the church at Philippi we find this beautifully demonstrated. That is the first of several aspects related to the Philippian church which we must take note of and learn its lesson.

Household Salvation

The second aspect or lesson we need to take notice of and learn is this. When the gospel was preached, Lydia and her household all believed and were baptized. The same thing happened to the jailer: not only did the jailer believe but his whole household also came to the Lord, and they too were all baptized. Here again, these instances of salvation demonstrate another important principle, that of household salvation. This principle, in fact, was established by God in relation to what happened in the Old Testament time when He delivered the children of Israel out of Egypt.

God had instructed every Jewish family to prepare a lamb—a lamb for each family. Yes, it is quite true that on the night of their deliverance from Egypt only the firstborn would be killed, but the firstborn simply represented the whole household. A lamb was slain for each family, the blood was put on the door post and the lintel, and the whole family—not just the firstborn but the whole family—had to gather together inside the house behind the door under the blood. There the whole household was to eat the lamb. And at midnight they were instructed to go out; and so the whole household and not merely the firstborn went out. And thus we see that in Old Testament typology household salvation was the principle of salvation; namely, that if anyone in the house is saved, there is a promise attached to that event: believe in the Lord Jesus and you shall be saved, you and your entire household. Yet it needs to be made clear here that this does not mean if someone in the family believes in the Lord Jesus, that all the members of the household automatically are also saved without their having to believe as well. No; it does not mean that.

We read in Acts 16:31 "Believe on the Lord Jesus and thou shalt be saved." Every one of us must believe. If you do not believe, and even though salvation is for the household, you will not be saved; but if you believe, you shall be saved. Moreover, God has promised you the salvation of your entire household; which is to say that if one gets saved, it is the responsibility of the one in the family who had believed in the Lord to go to Him, claim God's promise, and be a faithful witness in the household. If we believe and are faithful, we will find that God's promise is always true. Yet His promise does not come to us automatically. There is a responsibility on our side.

Have you as a believer in the Lord ever prayed for the members of your family? Let us say that you are saved but perhaps other members of your family have not come to the Lord yet; it is your responsibility to pray for them, claim the promise, and also bear a good testimony by living before them as a true disciple of Christ. God is faithful. I can cite case after case where whole families have come to the Lord because the first family member saved was thereafter faithful. In the thought of God, salvation is indeed for the entire household. We can therefore claim that promise of His before the Lord.

Labor of Love

There is another lesson we can learn from the life of the church in Philippi. This church began with a labor of love having been exhibited. From the moment Lydia was saved there was love which arose within her—a ministry of hospitality. She loved those who were the Lord's, and she could not accept the thought of Paul and his companions staying in an inn. She had a big house, and immediately she opened it and constrained Paul and his companions to come there and stay. Said Lydia to these servants of God: "If you truly regard me as being faithful to the Lord, then you have to come." That is love being demonstrated. The church in Philippi began with a labor of love. The same expression of love occurred with the jailer. He led Paul and Silas out from the dungeon, washed their wounds, and set a table of food before them. We see an immediate expression of love there. Hence, love marked the church's beginning in Philippi. It was not merely love expressed with the lips; it was an act of love, the service of love; and this that marked the Philippian church is what should mark every church of God.

Wherever there is an expression of the church of God its members need to love one another. That is the new commandment which the Lord gave to us: "Love one another as I have loved you" (see John 13:34). And we know that the Lord loved us with action; He loved us to the extent of giving himself up for us. And He commands us to likewise love with deeds and not just with words, and to love the brethren to the extent of giving up our lives for them. Such is what the life of the church is, and this is that to which we really need to take heart. Oh, that the love of Christ may so constrain us (cf. II Corinthians 5:14a) that we—like the church at Philippi—cannot but show love to all the brothers and sisters.

Travail and Suffering

The church in Philippi can teach us a further lesson, for it was born out of the travail of Paul and Silas. As was earlier discussed in the second message in this series, in birth there is always travail (cf. Genesis 3:16a). Today, people try to have birth without pain, but as a matter of fact birth is always accompanied by travail. So, too, the birth of a church comes forth through travail; yet, not only through the travail of the Lord Jesus on the cross but also through the suffering of God's servants. Moreover, not only did Paul and Silas suffer for the sake of faith, as we learn from the book of Acts; but also, by reading Paul's Letter to the Philippians we learn that that church was suffering for the faith as well. Wrote the apostle: "You have received grace not only in believing in the Lord, but also in suffering for Him" (see 1:29). Furthermore, wrote Paul, "You brethren have the same conflict which you have observed in me" (see v.30).

If we really believe and are faithful to the faith of the Lord Jesus, there is bound to be conflict. For the world will rise up and try to persecute us because the church is separated from it. Out of every nation, people, tongue and tribe, God has called out a people to himself. We are separated from the world by the faith of the gospel and hence we shall encounter conflict. The enemy of God will not allow us to go on smoothly; there will be much conflict occurring. Yes, Paul and Silas suffered for the faith, and even the church in Philippi had been given grace not only to believe but also to suffer. To believe on the Lord Jesus and to suffer for Him—that is grace. Do we suffer for the name of Jesus?

Sufferings can be of various kinds. We may not suffer physically by persecution, such as being cast into prison or being scourged. But if we really believe in the Lord and are faithful to our faith, we will suffer because it is with much tribulation that we must enter the kingdom of God (Acts 14:22). Sufferings and trials mature and perfect us and strengthen us (James 1:2-4 mg. NASB).

The church in Philippi did not only experience good times together; they also suffered for the name of Christ; and through that suffering the church was strengthened. That is another lesson we can and must learn from the life of this church: Do we have the will to suffer? Are we willing to give up ourselves? Are we willing to give up the world? Are we faithful to the Lord in following Him all the way?

Paul was in Philippi for just a short period because he was cast out by that city's authorities; but when he departed, he left someone behind. He and Silas and Timothy went on, but he left behind Luke, "the beloved physician" (cf. Colossians 4:14a). When we think of a physician, we may think of one who is so technical that he has no emotion, but Luke was called the beloved physician; he was full of love. Luke was left behind at Philippi to help with the young church, and he was with them for years. He did not rejoin Paul again until towards the end of Paul's third missionary journey in 58 A.D. (Acts 20:5). So with Luke in their midst helping them, no wonder the church in Philippi was one of love. It was full of love.

The Good Relationship between Church and Workers

A further lesson to be learned has to do with the Philippian church's relationship with God's servant-workers. We come to know quite a lot about the life of the church in Philippi because we have a letter that was written to its believers by Paul from a Roman prison in 63 A.D. First of all, I would like to mention that this letter was one of love. There was such an intimate loving relationship between Paul and the church in Philippi. Paul loved the believers there so much; for he wrote that he "longed for them all with the bowels (or affection; literally: inward parts) of Christ Jesus" (see 1:8). In response, the church in Philippi loved Paul quite much as well. They not only prayed for him and supported him at the beginning of his ministry there (1:5, 7, 19b), but after he left Macedonia, the Philippian church was the only one that supported Paul with financial help; in fact, twice the Philippian saints sent financial aid to him while he was at Thessalonica (4:14-16). Even when Paul was in a Roman prison, from whence he wrote this letter (4:22), and after so many years in it, they commissioned Epaphroditus to go to him with material help and serve the apostle (2:25, 30; 4:18b). There was thus a good relationship between the work and its workers on the one hand and the church on the other.

In our day we find many places where the workers and the church are in conflict, with many problems arising as a result. The workers try to control the church and the church tries to control the workers. A power struggle ensues and thus there are many problems. But in Philippi, the relationship was quite good between the church and the work and workers. All was in such good and proper order.

Humanly speaking the church in Philippi was started by Paul, but Paul did not control them. As is indicated throughout his entire letter, he prayed for them and helped them in whatever way he could. Even though he could not be there personally because he was in a Roman prison, he nonetheless wrote them. He was always concerned about them, and this was reciprocated by the church in Philippi. From the very first day they had stood with Paul in the preaching of the gospel (see again 1:5). Even while Paul was a prisoner in Rome for the defense of the gospel, the Philippian believers were participants with him (again, see 1:7). We hence see that from the beginning to the end, and even after many years had passed, they had stood firmly with Paul in the gospel without any let up. It was such a good relationship through and through.

What a lesson for us to learn in our day! If we examine Christianity today, we shall find that this is a much needed lesson to be learned. In one sense the work and the church are separated; but in another sense, they are divided but not separated. The workers are sent out by the Lord and they are guided by the Holy Spirit, but they are not controlled by any church or sent out by any church. They look to the Lord for their supply and they serve the Lord. The church, on the other hand, is not controlled by the workers, yet those in the church are one with the work of God. They support the work with prayer and with help. So the two—the church and the workers—really labor together. There is no conflict but they both labor together as one. And that is why the gospel was able to be extended so rapidly in the first century. It was a good relationship.

The Secret of Paul's Christian Life

As was indicated earlier, this Letter to the Philippians is a love letter, and because of that love relationship which existed between the apostle and the Philippian church, Paul was able to pour out his heart to them. Everyone who reads this letter immediately recognizes that this is a letter which reveals Paul as a person more than any other extant letter he ever wrote. He was able to really open himself up to the Philippians and say, "This is what I am." He unveiled to them the secret of his life—which is yet another lesson we can learn from the founding of this particular church. What is the secret of Paul's life? In his Letter to the Philippians he said, "For me to live is Christ" (1:21). That is the secret. The reason Paul could live as he did was simply because for him to live was Christ. And in chapter 2:5 he wrote, "Have the mind of Christ." Not only did he have the life of Christ, he also had the mind of Christ, which is characterized by selflessness and humility. Then in 3:10ff. Paul shows his readers his passion in life: to gain Christ. And finally, in 4:11a-13 the apostle reveals the secret of overcoming in every circumstance of life: "I have learned the secret that I can do all things through Him who empowers me." Now this is Christian living, this is Christian life; and Paul shared the secret with the Philippian believers whom he so greatly loved.

The Flaw in the Philippian Church

The church in Philippi was not perfect. You cannot find a perfect church on this earth; indeed, as some people have frankly declared: "It cannot be perfect as long as I am there." Yes, the Philippian church was one of love, no doubt about it, and the saints there stood with Paul from the beginning to the end of the gospel. There was much about them to be commended; and, in fact, you actually do not find any flaw in that church being mentioned by Paul in his letter until you come to the letter's very last chapter. By contrast, in reading Paul's

Letter to the Galatians you immediately see what was wrong with them. In his Letter to the Philippians, however, one cannot find any flaw until the end of it is reached, and even then, Paul only hints at it. He did not even characterize it as being a flaw, though it certainly was. For here was a church of love, a church firmly standing for the faith, one that stood in the conflict of the faith for the gospel, a church that stood for the gospel of Jesus Christ and was most willing to suffer for it. Yet there was in fact a flaw there. The flaw was what existed between two leading sisters, Euodia and Syntyche, who were Paul's co-workers who had helped him in the furtherance of the gospel. They were very zealous for the Lord and were apparently greatly gifted; nevertheless, there had developed a rivalry between these two women (4:2-3a).

In the world there is rivalry, a striving with one another for glory. But in the church there should never be such a thing. If we see any brother or sister being used by the Lord more than we, we should be happy about it. We should thank God for it because we are members one of another. If one is glorified, then we are all glorified. However, we are still human beings. Even in the church at Philippi that was a church of love—whose believers loved the Lord, were most zealous in laboring for Him and for the gospel—somehow, there developed a rivalry between these two women. Who between them had the greater influence? When the one looked at the other and saw that she was used more by the Lord, she was jealous, and vice versa. They each tried to create an influence among the saints for themselves. They did indeed love the Lord and the saints there; they even may have been willing to give up their lives; but something negative had happened between these two servants of God. And hence, that is why Paul at the very beginning of his Letter to the Philippians, prayed for the church. He never prayed a general prayer but always prayed very specifically, going directly to the target. So let us notice what he said in praying for the church in Philippi: "And this I pray, that your love may increase and abound more and more in full knowledge and all intelligence" (1:9), "so that ye may distinguish the things that differ" (1:10a ASV), "in order that ye may be pure and without offence for Christ's day" (1:10b).

Now we often say that love is blind. If you know too much—say, about another person—you are not able to love anymore. But spiritual love is different. Spiritual love has its eyes wide open. It is to be in full knowledge and all intelligence. Now love itself cannot be increased because God is love, and therefore, the love of Christ in you is complete. But love can be increased in both knowledge and intelligence. Just think of that! Having full knowledge refers to one's having awareness of the eternal purpose of God. And possessing all intelligence has reference to one's spiritual discernment. And it is with that kind of knowledge and intelligence that can enable you to see or distinguish between the things that differ (NASB); can enable you to "judge of and approve the things that are more excellent, in order that [you] may be pure and without offence for Christ's day" (Darby). What does all that mean? It means that though there is love in you, you will know what ought to be loved, how to love, and where love is to be applied. You will know and be able to discern or distinguish between the things that differ. You do not simply love and love and love blindly. You love according to the will of God and do so with discernment, being able to judge whether such love is of the flesh or of the spirit.

In the church at Philippi those two sisters did have love, most certainly, but evidently they were lacking in full knowledge of the eternal purpose of God, which is Christ. They in their self-life began to slip back into the flesh and seek for vainglory (cf. 2:3a). Instead of esteeming the other as more excellent than each of them were, they had lost that spirit of humility, the spirit of the Lamb (cf. 2:3b-4). That is what is needed which will enable one to know the things that differ; you will be able to discern the difference. Now that is what the believers in Philippi lacked. They observed how these two sisters were so zealous for the Lord, and were being so greatly used by Him, and yet they were at odds with each other, perhaps striving secretly against each other. Somehow a cloud had spread over the whole assembly as a consequence. These two sisters did not know what to do; they lacked that discernment which is so essential in being "pure and without offence." Not only these two sisters but all the brothers and sisters needed to have their love abound more and more in full knowledge and all intelligence, in order that they might discern the things that differ, in order that there might be further and deeper dealings with one's flesh so that they would be pure and without offense for the day of Christ. Let us notice that in this letter Paul made reference a number of times to Christ's day or the day of Christ Jesus. That is the day we are all looking forward to when we shall appear before Him at the judgment seat of Christ (II Corinthians 5:10).

So Paul was gently telling these two sisters: "You love, but you do not have full knowledge and all intelligence. You do not discern between the things that differ. Self is still there; flesh is still there. You therefore need to be dealt with by the cross, and then you will have the mind of Christ and you both will be one" (cf. 2:2). Out of his love for the Philippian church, and though he was unable to speak to them directly, Paul wrote to them and mentioned his prayer for them to the effect that their love would truly abound more and more in full knowledge and all intelligence, and the result would be "to God's glory and praise" (1:11b).

We thank God that though we are not perfect, there is hope. The Lord will not allow us to remain in ignorance. He will still exhort, instruct, persuade, and beseech us, in order to bring us into that place where we will be to God's glory and praise.

Dear Lord, we do pray that the lessons Thou hast given us in the life of the church in Philippi may be well learned by heart. Lord, we pray that Thy word will not fall upon hard and stony ground but that it may fall upon ground which has been tilled so that it may patiently bear fruit a hundred fold unto Thyself. Lord, may glory be unto Thee in the church. In Thy name we pray. Amen.

Chapter Seven

THE CHURCH IN THESSALONICA

 Acts 17:1-10a—*And having journeyed through Amphipolis and Apollonia, they [Paul, Silas, and Timothy] came to Thessalonica, where was the synagogue of the Jews. And according to Paul's custom he went in among them, and on three sabbaths reasoned with them from the scriptures, opening and laying down that the Christ must have suffered and risen up from among the dead, and that this is the Christ, Jesus whom I announce to you. And some of them believed, and joined themselves to Paul and Silas, and of the Greeks who worshipped, a great multitude, and of the chief women not a few. But the Jews having been stirred up to jealousy, and taken to themselves certain wicked men of the lowest rabble, and having got a crowd together, set the city in confusion; and having beset the house of Jason sought to bring them out to the people; and not having found them, dragged Jason and certain brethren before the politarchs, crying out, These men that have set the world in tumult, are come here also, whom Jason has received; and these all do contrary to the decrees of Caesar, saying, that there is another king, Jesus. And they troubled the crowd and the politarchs when they heard these things. And having taken security of Jason and the rest, they let them go. But the brethren immediately sent away, in the night, Paul and Silas to Berea.*

We have been looking into the life of the early churches—especially those that are recorded in the book of Acts—to see how those church believers lived their lives together, to learn what testimony they brought to the world, to discover in what special areas they were blessed, and to note in what respect they were warned. And the reason for all this is that we may learn from them the lessons which the Holy Spirit wants to teach us today. So we will continue on with the life of the church in Thessalonica.

The Birth of the Thessalonian Church

After Paul and Silas were asked to leave the city of Philippi, they traveled on to Thessalonica, which was about a hundred miles from Philippi. It too was in the Roman province of Macedonia, and in fact was its capital city at that time. It was not only a political, but also a commercial, center. And unlike at Philippi there was a synagogue there as well. Paul's custom was to enter the synagogue to preach the glad tidings of the Lord Jesus because the people who attended the synagogues were at least familiar with the Old Testament Scriptures. Therefore, here at Thessalonica Paul went to the synagogue and reasoned with the attendees according to the Scriptures as to how Christ must suffer first and then be glorified; further, that this Christ was none other than Jesus, whom he announced to them. Thus, for three Sabbaths Paul and Silas attended the synagogue and argued with those present from the Scriptures that Jesus is the Christ, that He is indeed the Messiah whom God had promised to His chosen people. As a result, a few of the Jews believed, and so they joined themselves to Paul and Silas. Moreover, from among the worshiping Gentiles a great multitude believed in the Lord Jesus, and quite a few of the city's chief women also believed.

Now when God's word was preached in Thessalonica, Paul noted in his first letter to them that it had not come to them in

The Church in Thessalonica

word only but also in power and in the Holy Spirit and with much assurance (I Thessalonians 1:5a). The word was preached with the power of the Holy Spirit; and the word was backed up by the lives of the preachers: the way Paul and his companions had lived before the people reinforced the word which they had preached (1:5b, 2:1ff.). And because of this, many came to the Lord in a very short time. As a matter of fact, these people, noted Paul, had welcomed the gospel message despite intense suffering, and did so with the joy given by the Holy Spirit (1:6b); and because of that, the news spread all over Macedonia, even to neighboring Achaia. People there had become aware of how Paul, Silas and Timothy had entered into their midst, how the word was preached, how God's servants had lived among them, and how, in the midst of great tribulation, the people had received the word of God with the joy of the Holy Spirit; and so, their faith was reported everywhere (1:7-8).

This, however, had aroused the jealousy of the Jews, who made use of some of that society's lowest rabble, and created a great confusion in the city. They surrounded the house of Jason where Paul, Silas and Timothy were staying, but the crowd could not find them there. So instead they dragged Jason and some brethren before the city's magistrates. They accused Paul and his co-workers of being those who had troubled the whole world and had now come to Thessalonica preaching against the decrees of Caesar and announcing that there was another king—one whom they called Jesus. Finally, the magistrates made Jason and the brethren post bond and released them. But that very night the brethren sent Paul and Silas away and they went on to Berea. Such was the beginning of the church in Thessalonica.

The Travail of the Apostles

The church in Thessalonica was born through the travail of the apostles. They suffered in that city. Even before they came to Thessalonica, they had suffered in Philippi; nevertheless, in spite of their suffering there they entered Thessalonica and faithfully and bravely proclaimed the gospel of Jesus Christ. And hence, the church in Thessalonica could be said to have been born through their travail. This is always true with God's church everywhere. Wherever the church of God comes into being, it comes through the travail of some of God's people. A church is never organized but is always born, and there will be no birth without travail. This was true in the time of the apostles and this is still true today.

Not only did the apostles travail to bring forth the Thessalonian church, but those who became the church there actually suffered a great deal themselves. It was in tribulation that they received and welcomed the gospel of Jesus Christ with the joy of the Holy Spirit. A church that is born under such conditions is usually stronger than a church that is born peacefully because probably those latter brethren are not so totally separated from the world. But if people come to the Lord under persecution or tribulation, their separation from the world is more complete and their dedication to the Lord is more absolute. As a matter of fact, suffering is good for us all.

We know a great deal about the church in Thessalonica even though we have only a few verses about its birth in the book of Acts. The reason we know its condition and the lives of its saints is because of the two letters which Paul wrote to them from the Greek city of Corinth. When Paul was in the midst of the Thessalonians, he was as a mother to them; he cared much for those young believers (I Thessalonians 2:7). He loved them to the extent that he said he would not only preach the gospel to them but he would gladly give up his life for them (I Thessalonians 2:8). What a love there was in the heart of the apostle Paul! Of all the extant letters we have which he wrote, those sent to the Philippians, to Philemon, and to the church in Thessalonica are the most compassionate love letters which Paul ever wrote. How it is hoped that all God's servants would be like the apostle Paul—that there would be a similar love manifested among His servants towards the churches of Christ; that there would be such a willingness to give, to spend, and to be spent on behalf of the brethren in the churches. Yet, in our consideration together today I do not wish us to be focused on the worker but on the life of the church in Thessalonica.

Of all the extant letters of Paul which we have today, I and II Thessalonians were the first two letters written by him to the various churches. He wrote these particular ones in 52 and 53 A.D., only a few months after he had left Thessalonica.

Thoroughly and Soundly Saved

From the first of these two letters to the Thessalonians we learn, first of all, that those who had believed in the Lord Jesus there were thoroughly and soundly saved. They were mostly Gentiles, and had been idol worshipers as well; but they then had turned to God from their idols to serve the true and living God and to await the coming of God's Son whom God had raised from the dead—indeed, the One who is to be their Deliverer from the coming wrath (1:9b-10). In other words, in terms of sequential timings, it could be said that they turned away from idols to God—that was their past; they henceforth served the true and living God—that was their present; and they awaited the second coming of the Lord Jesus—that was their future. Therefore, their turning from idols was complete; and their turning to God was absolute.

Many today turn to God, but they do not serve Him. The Thessalonian believers turned away from the idols which they had previously served and turned to God, the true and living One, and immediately they began to serve Him. Every brother and sister there served God with their whole heart. That is something highly commendable, and that is a characteristic which ought to be true of all of us today. We ought to say—and mean it: "We are saved to serve." We are not saved merely to enjoy the blessings or to be saved simply for ourselves. We are saved with a purpose in view—to serve God and serve His purpose. Otherwise, we are being self-centered and selfish even when we believe in the Lord Jesus. Hence, we see that after these Thessalonians turned away from their useless, powerless idols and turned to the one true and living God, they immediately began to serve Him with their whole heart.

Not only that, but they awaited with expectant hearts for the return coming of the Lord Jesus to the earth (see again 1:10a). Here they were in great affliction and in "much tribulation" (1:6b); what, therefore, could give them the endurance they needed most? Would it not be the blessed hope of every Christian? As the church of God, we have a blessed hope; and our blessed hope is the coming again of the Lord Jesus. Inasmuch as God has taken us out of this world, we are now aliens so far as this world is concerned (John 15:19), and as aliens we will suffer (John 15:19c, 20b). Hence, suffering should be no strange phenomenon to believers (cf. I Peter 4:12-13). It is something we should expect because we do not any longer belong to the world. The world will hate us because it first hated the Lord Jesus (John 15:18, 20b). But thank God, we have a blessed hope, and that hope of ours is not on this earth; on the contrary, our hope is the coming from heaven of our Lord Jesus, and so we shall be with Him forever. Thus we see that the Thessalonian church had in their Christian experience all these important phases—the past was a complete separation, the present was an absolute devotion, and the future was centered upon a blessed hope. That is what we find, first of all, in the church at Thessalonica.

Three Essentials to Our Christian Life

Paul said in I Corinthians 13:13a: "Now abide faith, hope, and love." There are three things which are most essential to our Christian living, and these are faith, love, and hope. We find that from the very beginning the Thessalonian church had these three important elements. They had the "work of faith," the "labour of love," and the "enduring constancy of hope" (I Thessalonians 1:3).

Faith

Of course, we know faith is most basic to us Christians. Without faith it is impossible to please God (Hebrews 11:6a). Everyone who comes to the Lord must have faith: and we believe that God is, and that He is the rewarder of all who seek after Him (Hebrews 11:6b). It is by faith that we are justified (Romans 3:28b). Everything is based on faith, on believing—believing, first of all, in the Lord Jesus as the Christ, the Son of the living God; otherwise, we are not the children of God (John 1:12). So faith is basic to us; but it is a matter of our living from faith to faith (Romans 1:17AV, ASV mgn). It is not that once upon a time we believed, but then we merely remain there in that condition or level of faith. Not so; faith must grow and increase. It is to be from faith to faith.

Not only must that be true of us who believe, but such faith is perfected by works. We realize, of course, that we are not justified by works (cf. Ephesians 2:9) because our works—the works of our natural man—are nothing but filthy rags before God (Isaiah 64:6a). We have no righteousness of our own. No one can be justified by his works or by his merits. We are only justified by faith in the Lord Jesus and in His finished work on the cross. Now that is very fundamental.

On the other hand, after we have believed in the Lord Jesus, how are we going to prove or demonstrate that our faith is genuine, that our faith is real? In his epistle James tells us that we are justified by works (2:24); but it is by works of faith (cf. James 2:20-24), not works of the natural man, since faith without works is like a body without a spirit (2:26). You say you believe, but the demons also believe and they tremble

(2:19). How are you going to prove your faith in the Lord Jesus? It is by works. Ephesians 2:8 says we are saved by grace, through faith; and it is not of ourselves; it is a gift of God. Even faith is a gift of God. But Ephesians 2 goes on to say that we are God's workmanship, and because of that, we are saved to do the works which God has—in preparation—foreordained for us to do (v.10). The Thessalonian church not only had the faith, but they had the *works* of faith. They demonstrated and expressed their faith by their works.

Love

Moreover, there was love exhibited among these saints. The church in Thessalonica not only loved the Lord Jesus, who had loved them so much that He gave himself for them, but they also loved the brethren; they loved one another. There was brotherly love in their midst, and there was the *labor* of love. Love is an emotion, and thus it is invisible; but it is made visible by labor. If you really love, then you are willing to labor; you are willing to serve your brothers and sisters in a variety of ways. If there is genuine Christian love, there is nothing too lowly for you to do for your brethren. This young church, which at this moment was only a few months old, manifested in practical terms the labor of love.

Hope

Not only that essential element, they in addition had the enduring constancy of hope. In the midst of "much tribulation" these saints in Thessalonica were filled with the "joy of the Holy Spirit" (1:6b, 7a). How was this so?—for it is natural when you are in tribulation to feel sorrowful, to be grieved; but instead of exhibiting that reaction they were filled with the joy of the Holy Spirit because they had a blessed hope. They knew the Lord was coming soon, and so they cast their anchor in heaven instead of on the earth. In the first, second and third centuries, whenever the church passed through periods of tribulation and persecution, they would greet each other whenever they saw each other with the words: "The Lord is coming!" That was their confident greeting.

We are now at the end of this age, full of difficult days; and what is our blessed hope? We need to greet each other with: "The Lord is coming!" It shows that our home is not here but up above. We are waiting for Him. The Thessalonian believers had that endurance which comes from the blessed hope.

A Lurking Danger

Let us be aware, however, that as a church grows older, there is a danger. Let us recall what happened to the church in Ephesus. It had had a glorious beginning, and the church continued to flourish even up to the time when Paul wrote his letter to the Ephesian believers while he was in prison. They constituted a church of undying love; but by the end of the first century after the Ephesian church had existed for quite a number of years, we find that a detrimental change had happened. This we learn from the book of Revelation. The Christians there still had works, still had labor, and still had patience; but it was no longer the work of faith, the labor of love, and the patience of hope (2:2a). Briefly stated, the inward springs were missing, and that is always a danger which can overtake a church.

At the beginning, when saints are young and fresh in the Lord, there is something quite living that is present in the church. People truly have that inner power and motivation within them to pursue after faith, love, and hope. But as weeks and months and years pass by, and though the believers in the church may outwardly still manifest works, labor, patience and endurance, there comes a time when the Lord must declare to the church: "I am against you because you have lost your first love" (2:4). How very important it is, therefore, that we renew our faith, love and hope before the Lord. The only way we can do this is to draw near to Him, commune with Him, and allow the Holy Spirit to touch us and reveal wherein we have fallen (2:5a) so that we will not continue on routinely but that there will be reignited within us that inner motivating fire to once again have that faith, hope and love. This is that which we need to frequently—perhaps even daily—return to the Lord about. Let us be under His light constantly to see if that living faith is still there behind our works, to see if that first love is still there behind our labor, and to see if that living hope is still there behind our patience and endurance.

Thank God for the lives of those in the church at Thessalonica that were continually fresh and living. No wonder that the word concerning their faith spread abroad, not only in Macedonia and Achaia, but that wherever Paul and his fellow workers went, people had already heard what had happened in Thessalonica (1:7-10). May the Lord really help us in this regard.

Functioning Together

Within only a few months of its birth, all believers in the church at Thessalonica were functioning together. Paul had left them after a short period of time, so these Christians were on their own, as it were. But because the Lord was there, because the Holy Spirit was in their midst, and because they honored the Lord as their Head, they learned to take up responsibility for one another. Humanly speaking we would say they had been left as orphans, for nobody was actually taking care of them, not even Timothy. Yes, Timothy was later sent back to see how they were faring (3:2); in reality, though, they had been left on their own. More than likely in our day, if something like this were to occur, all the brothers and sisters would moan and say among themselves: "Our spiritual parent(s) have left us as orphans and we do not know what to do. Let's secure a pastor who will come and minister to us and do all the work for us." Is that not what would probably happen? That was not the case, however, in the early church. Back then, the apostles would go to a place, people would be saved, they would gather them together for worship of the Lord, and ultimately the apostles would leave and go elsewhere, leaving the saints in the care of the Lord and not in the care of man. Were the apostles to stay there, those new believers would probably have depended on the apostles and would probably never have grown up. They would never have become responsible since those apostles would have been taking care of them.

As the church of God each and every member of the body of Christ is responsible for the whole body. The church in Thessalonica, which was but a few months old, had learned to care for one another, to encourage one another; even as Paul wrote in I Thessalonians chapter 5: "But we exhort you, brethren, admonish the disorderly, comfort the faint-hearted, sustain the weak, be patient towards all" (v.14). One can therefore infer from this that all the brothers and sisters were encouraged to function in helping one another. How? Such mutual functioning was under the headship of Christ.

Church Leadership Manifested to All by the Holy Spirit

At the same time, again within a short time period, the Holy Spirit had already manifested those who would be in leadership. For also in I Thessalonians chapter 5 we can read this: "But we beg you, brethren, to know those who labour among you, and take the lead among you in the Lord, and admonish you, and to regard them exceedingly in love on account of their work" (vv.12-13a). One can therefore conclude that these brethren in Thessalonica had been soundly saved. Much of our problem today stems from the fact that, yes, we are saved, but we are barely saved. If believers are soundly saved and are under the headship of Christ, then our Head will most certainly take care of His body. Can you at all imagine that Christ would leave His flock without care?!? He is responsible for them, is He not?

Within a very short period God had already raised up some among the Thessalonian church members who were able to admonish the saints there, to labor among them, and to lead them on in the Lord. They were not appointed by man but were manifested to all in the church by the Holy Spirit. There was no position and no title, but there was body function taking place. It was a work of love. To lead, to encourage, to exhort, to strengthen, to care are descriptions of various works of love. Today, we look at leadership as those who bear a title or position or something that needs to be ordained or appointed by man; but back in those early days, it was not so. Everybody in the church recognized it for what it was: a labor of love; and because of this labor of love from those who gave themselves to the church, the other brothers and sisters paid respect to them. It was not respect paid towards a position but a respect paid towards their labor of love. It was a respect of love, by which is meant that the brothers and sisters loved those who led because of their leaders' work of love among them. In short, it was as Paul had expressed it in his letter to the church brethren there: a showing of a "regard [towards] them exceedingly in love on account of their work [of love]" (5:13a).

How differently we find the situation in the church today. In the Christian church today this matter of leadership is a problem everywhere. How is church leadership produced? Speaking theoretically, we know the Holy Spirit will manifest church leaders; but after they become manifested, they are not recognized because everybody wants to be the head and not be content to be the tail. There is such conflict between leadership and the body. But in a normal church there is harmony. On the one hand, those in leadership serve with love; and on the other hand, those who are being served respect those in leadership with love. What a beautiful picture that is! Now that was the life of the church in Thessalonica.

Paul's Emphasis for the Thessalonian Church

Though Paul was with the Christians in Thessalonica for only a very short period, there were two matters which he especially stressed while he was in their midst. The first of these two was sanctification, and the second, the return coming of the Lord.

Sanctification

We learn from I and II Thessalonians that when Paul was in their midst, he told them very plainly that the will of God for them was their sanctification (4:3a, 2:13b). God had called them not to uncleanness but to holiness (4:7). Today we tend to separate, if we can, justification from sanctification. We initially preach justification: "You are justified by faith" (see again Romans 3:28b). Thank God for that. Then we leave the matter there for perhaps a year or some years before we then speak about sanctification. Actually, though, justification and sanctification cannot be separated. As a matter of fact, we are not even sure which comes first!

Now we would probably claim that justification comes first; but in I Corinthians 6:11 Paul is found mentioning sanctification before justification: "And these things were some of you; but ye have been washed, but ye have been sanctified, but ye have been justified in the name of the Lord Jesus, and by the Spirit of our God." Here the apostle put sanctification before justification. So which comes first? Neither, since they come together. When we are justified we are sanctified, because to be sanctified simply means "to be set apart for God." You are not justified in order that you may be your own; you are justified that you may be set apart for God. That is sanctification. Hence, you are separated to God from the very first day of your salvation.

In one of his letters to the Thessalonians Paul presented sanctification not so much as a doctrine but more as a matter of practical experience—that is to say, not so much in terms of a position before God but in terms of a condition before Him (I Thessalonians 4:3-8). This was because the city of Thessalonica was primarily a Gentile community that was quite immoral, and thus those who believed in the Lord Jesus were mostly Gentiles. They came from a very immoral background, and after they were saved, they were separated from the world. So Paul taught them that they needed to be wholly sanctified—in body, in soul, and in spirit (5:23).

We, too, need to be sanctified wholly. Not only is our spirit separated unto God, even in our soul we are to be sanctified: that is to say, our will, our mind and our emotion have to be delivered from the world and from self so that Christ may be expressed through these faculties of our soul. And even our body needs to be sanctified in order to prove to the world that we are indeed a purified people.

In reviewing church history we may discover that one of the reasons for the success of the Methodists in their early days was most likely because John Wesley had emphasized sanctification by faith. Let us therefore ask ourselves: Are we separated? Are we different? Is our spirit, soul, and body being totally sanctified so that we may be blameless in the day of Christ? (5:23b-c) From the very beginning of Paul's relationship with the Thessalonian believers he had emphasized sanctification as a condition, as a practical reality; and that strengthened the people there.

The Return Coming of the Lord

Paul's second special emphasis concerned the return coming of the Lord. The saints in Thessalonica had been thrust into great tribulation, for we have seen that they had believed in the Lord Jesus in the midst of great suffering, and their blessed hope, as we also learned, lay in the second coming of the Lord Jesus. So in these two letters Paul wrote much about Jesus' second coming. As a matter of fact, that is the only way by which we will be kept in faithfulness to the Lord when experiencing tribulation.

The Day of Christ

In Paul's first Thessalonian letter his emphasis concerned "Christ's day" or the day of Christ (see Philippians 1:6, 10; 2:16; I Corinthians 1:8; 5:5). One day we shall all appear before Christ as the family of God. Christ shall come and we will all be gathered before Him; that is the day of Christ. It is a day to which we should look forward; unfortunately, however, it will also be a day that some shall be fearful of because as we all gather before Christ, that will be the time when we must stand before His judgment seat (II Corinthians 5:10).

Now during those few months between the time of Paul's departure from Thessalonica and the writing of his two letters some of the Thessalonian saints had died, and the church there had not fully understood the teaching concerning the coming of the Lord (I Thessalonians 4:13). So they now had a mistaken idea that those who had recently died would miss the blessing of the Lord's return coming; and hence, Paul tried to comfort them by means of his first letter (cf. 4:18).

It is true that we need to wait for the coming of the Lord in our lifetime. As a matter of fact, from the first century up till now, every generation of those who have loved the Lord have waited for the Lord to come in their lifetime. This attitude is correct. Even though the Lord has not yet come, our constant attitude should be that of looking forward to His return in our lifetime. That is what God wants us to do, but for reasons perhaps only known to Him, Jesus has delayed His return and some saints in Thessalonica had slept—that is, had died. Those

Thessalonian believers were looking forward with great intensity of heart to the Lord's coming in their lifetime so as to be delivered out of all their problems and adverse circumstances, but some had meanwhile died and those who remained were discouraged. They thought that those who had died would miss the soon-to-occur blessing.

Paul therefore wrote to them saying that when the Lord comes, the trumpet will sound and those who are asleep in Christ Jesus will rise first. Those who are alive and remain (even some of *them* will already be gone) will be changed, and all will be caught up to the air to meet the Lord in the air to be with Him forever. That is the sum and substance regarding the day of Christ which Paul described in great detail in his first letter to the Thessalonian church (4:13-17), and this is the day to which we are all looking forward.

Oh, how Paul himself looked forward to that day when he—blameless—would see the Lord face to face and receive his reward (cf. II Timothy 4:6-8). But such is the day also that we should be fearful of, lest when we see Him we shall be put to shame (I John 2:28). May the Lord help us. Such was Paul's second subject of emphasis in his I Thessalonian letter.

The Day of the Lord

After a very short time period, Paul wrote another letter to the Thessalonian church. The reason for writing a second letter was because someone had sent a letter to the same church—but in the name of Paul—and telling them that "the day of the Lord" had already come (2:2). Now in the Scriptures the day of the Lord is different from the day of Christ. The day of the Lord has reference to a day of God's judgment. This actually is an Old Testament term. The day of the Lord or the day of Jehovah which one finds mentioned frequently throughout the Old Testament prophecies refers to a day of judgment. It is a day when God will come forth and judge. When this false letter came to the Thessalonians declaring that the day of the Lord had already come, and because these believers were experiencing tribulation, they thought God's judgment had come upon them and that therefore they had missed the blessing of Jesus' return to the earth. Hence Paul felt it necessary to write again to comfort them by telling them that the day of the Lord had not come yet.

The day of Christ is what all faithful believers in Jesus are looking forward to with great eagerness and joy. The day of the Lord, however, is a day of God's judgment, and it will not come until there is an apostasy—a falling away (2:3ff.). In Christianity there will occur an apostasy in the end-time: a majority of the people will fall away, there being only a minority who will be faithful in following the Lamb wheresoever He goes. Accordingly, there shall be a general falling away from the Lord. Are we almost in that day?

Paul next explained further in his second epistle to the Thessalonians. Then the man of sin, or the man of perdition, or the antichrist—wrote the apostle—will appear on the earth, and the Lord will come and kill him with the breath of His mouth (2:8). So by way of conclusion Paul in so many words said this: "Be comforted; the day of judgment has not yet come. This current tribulation of yours is not the judgment yet. It is but God's disguised love in preparing you for the day of Christ when we all shall see Him face to face" (cf. 2:15-17).

These two teachings were greatly stressed in those early days of God's church, and how we also need these two teachings in our day: the teaching on sanctification or holiness and that concerning the coming of the Lord; and if faithfully observed by us, we shall be prepared for the Lord Jesus' return.

Disciplined As Sons

Finally, there is the issue of discipline and Paul's warning. A church is not a church if there is no discipline. We may think that since everything in the church is to be seasoned with love, therefore, everything is allowed, all are free to do as they wish; and hence, there is no need for such a thing as discipline. But ask yourself: Can you have a home wherein no discipline is exercised, wherein everything is nothing but "a free-for-all"? If so, what kind of home is *that*? Let us realize that in the house of God, there is order, there is discipline.

There were people in the church at Thessalonica—perhaps only a few, but nonetheless there were some—who refused to work. They could work but they refused to have a job. They instead relied on the love of the brothers and sisters to supply their needs. And because they were lazy in hand, they became quite diligent in mouth; and hence, they became busybodies and caused problems in the church. In his letter Paul reminded the brethren: "Do you remember when I was with you? I worked with my hands day and night to set an example for you. This is the principle all should follow: No work, no eating. And if anyone refuses to hear this, then no one else in the church should keep company with him. Leave him alone until he feels ashamed; nevertheless, do not treat him as an enemy but continue to love him as a brother" (cf. 3:6-16).

There are those in the church in our day who do not want discipline. When discipline is exercised, they say there is no love there; but if there be no discipline, no love is there; for the book of Hebrews tells us that our heavenly Father chastens and disciplines us as sons *because He loves us* and wants us to grow into maturity. And hence, if He does not discipline us, we are as it were illegitimate children and not sons. Consequently, let us not despise the discipline of the Lord and let us not faint under discipline. It is by being chastened that we are made partakers of His holiness—that is, partakers of His divine nature. Yes, it is quite true that when we are disciplined, it is not a pleasant thing; but afterwards, it will bear the fruit of righteousness (12:5-11).

These are the various lessons which we can learn from the life of the church in Thessalonica. I firmly believe that though this expression of the church of God occurred nearly two thousand years ago, these lessons learned can be very living for us today.

Dear Lord, we thank Thee for giving us these two letters to the Thessalonians. We thank Thee for showing us through these letters and the book of Acts the life of the early church. We thank Thee for the encouragements and also the warnings we find in them. Lord, we pray that by Thy Holy Spirit Thou wilt teach us all the lessons we need to learn today. In Thy name we pray. Amen.

Chapter Eight

THE CHURCH IN CORINTH

Acts 18:1-11—And after these things, having left Athens, he [Paul] came to Corinth; and finding a certain Jew by name Aquila, of Pontus by race, just come from Italy, and Priscilla his wife, (because Claudius had ordered all the Jews to leave Rome,) came to them, and because they were of the same trade abode with them, and wrought. For they were tent-makers by trade. And he reasoned in the synagogue every sabbath, and persuaded Jews and Greeks. And when both Silas and Timotheus came down from Macedonia, Paul was pressed in respect of the word, testifying to the Jews that Jesus was the Christ. But as they opposed and spoke injuriously, he shook his clothes, and said to them, Your blood be upon your own head: I am pure; from henceforth I will go to the nations. And departing thence he came to the house of a certain man, by name Justus, who worshipped God, whose house adjoined the synagogue. But Crispus the ruler of the synagogue believed in the Lord with all his house; and many of the Corinthians hearing, believed, and were baptised. And the Lord said by vision in the night to Paul, Fear not, but speak and be not silent; because I am with thee, and no one shall set upon thee to injure thee; because I have much people in this city. And he remained there a year and six months, teaching among them the word of God.

> *I Corinthians 2:1-5—And I, when I came to you, brethren, came not in excellency of word, or wisdom, announcing to you the testimony of God. For I did not judge it well to know anything among you save Jesus Christ, and him crucified. And I was with you in weakness and in fear and in much trembling; and my word and my preaching, not in persuasive words of wisdom, but in demonstration of the Spirit and of power; that your faith might not stand in men's wisdom, but in God's power.*
>
> *II Corinthians 13:11-14—For the rest, brethren, rejoice; be perfected; be encouraged; be of one mind; be at peace; and the God of love and peace shall be with you. Salute one another with a holy kiss. All the saints salute you. The grace of the Lord Jesus Christ, and the love of God, and the communion of the Holy Spirit, be with you all.*

When the Lord Jesus was on earth, He lived in a physical body; and in that physical body He taught and He worked. After His death, resurrection, and ascension He took upon himself a mystical body on this earth—a body that is made up of all those who believe in Him. It is the church, the body of Christ; and in this mystical body Jesus continues to do and to teach. So our interest during these messages is to see how the Lord Jesus—the risen Head—lives in and through this mystical body of His.

Now throughout the book of Acts we read how this mystical body, the church, was established from city to city, starting from Jerusalem and continuing through all Judea, Samaria, and even to the end of the known world. At that time the end of the world was Rome and its Empire; and accordingly, in Acts we learn that the church ended up in Rome too. But we know, of course, that actually the book of Acts has no ending because the life of the church, the body of Christ, continues on even up to our very day as well, and it will continue until the return to the earth of Jesus her Head.

In view of this, therefore, whatever is recorded in God's word is there for our edification and also for our admonition; so as we read the various narratives describing how the churches in different places came to birth, lived, and witnessed for the Lord, I believe such a record is to be viewed as more than simply history of the first century church but that God placed such a record in His word for us to read so that we may learn important lessons from them. There are pitfalls which we should avoid, problems which we should know how to solve, and ways which we should learn to follow. So in our consideration together on these churches of the first century, my desire is not only for us to know some historical facts but also for us to learn from those brothers and sisters of ours who lived in that earlier age. In other words, I would like for us to learn how Christ lived through those earlier brethren in order that we may know how to allow Him to live through us corporately in our own day.

How the Church in Corinth Began

We earlier learned that during the second missionary journey of the apostle Paul, the Spirit of God did not allow him to remain in western Asia Minor, but he was led to cross the Aegean Sea into Europe. By this means the gospel began to be spread from the continent of Asia to that of Europe: first to Philippi and then to Thessalonica. In Acts 18 we are next told that after Paul left Athens he went onward to Corinth as part of his second missionary travel that in total would cover about three years—from 50 to 53 A.D.

Corinth at that time was the capital of the province of Achaia; it was very beautifully situated. It was a commercial city, and because of its commerce it became a very wealthy city.

Corinth was also famous as the patron city where were held the Isthmian Games which along with the Olympian Games were two of the four Panhellenic Games—the collective term for four separate sports festivals that had begun in ancient Greek times. It was a highly civilized city, but very corrupt and immoral; and drinking was a serious problem among its people.

Strangely, the city of Corinth had become famous at that time for two seemingly contradictory traits. One was its dissipated living; in fact, there was a well-known saying: "He lives like a Corinthian"—which meant a person lives a very corrupt, immoral life. But then there was a second saying which was reflective of the other trait: "He has the speaking of the Corinthians"—meaning that a person is eloquent in speech. The Corinthians were very famous for their eloquence: when speaking, they could frame ideas in a very logical and appealing manner. So, on the one hand, Corinthians lived very corrupt lives; on the other hand, they spoke very eloquently. Such was the cultural situation in the city of Corinth at that time.

Before Paul came into that city he had made a determination as he viewed Corinth from afar. What should he do in relation to the Corinthians when he arrived there? How should he approach them with the salvation message? He said he was determined that in their midst he would know nothing save Jesus Christ and Him crucified. Paul was determined not to match eloquence with eloquence, intelligence with intelligence, because he saw that what the Corinthians really needed was Jesus Christ and Him crucified. So that was his settled intention before he even entered the city.

When Paul first arrived, he was all by himself because Timothy had been sent to Thessalonica and Silas was still in Berea; but he somehow learned that there was a Christian married couple in the city—Aquila and Priscilla. This formerly Jewish couple had just come from Rome where Caesar Claudius had decreed that all Jews must leave Rome. We are told in history that the reason Claudius had issued the decree was

The Church in Corinth

because trouble had arisen among the Jews in Rome over the name, Chrestus, or Christus. This name, we know, has reference to Christ, and evidently the gospel of Jesus Christ had been brought to Rome by some people, which in turn had caused some turmoil among the Jewish community there. And hence, in order to bring an end to the trouble all Jews were ordered out of Rome.

Aquila and Priscilla were now Christians. We do not know how they became Christians, but we are told that probably they were among those who had attended Pentecost in Jerusalem and were possibly among the 3000 people who were saved on that memorable occasion. After they were saved, so goes the story, they returned to Rome; and probably they themselves were among those who had helped spread the good news, eventually causing the turmoil to erupt among the Jews. They and all the other Jews were thus ordered out of Rome, and so this couple had decided to go to Corinth.

Paul stayed with them because they were not only fellow Christians—even probably having become Christians before Paul—but they were engaged in the same trade. The education of the Jews involved not only study but also required every man to learn a trade. It so happened that Paul had learned the trade of tent-making. Aquila had also become a tent-maker, and hence Paul stayed with them and they worked together with their hands.

On the Sabbath Paul and Aquila and Priscilla would go to the synagogue, and the apostle would reason with the Jews about the gospel of Jesus Christ. But he mainly spent his days working with his hands. It was only on the Sabbath day that he would go to the synagogue to reason with the Jews; but after Silas and Timothy came down from Macedonia something happened, and Paul's heart was stirred. Indeed, he was pressed and constrained by the word of God; so he began to preach the gospel even more frequently and fervently—yet, not only on the Sabbath in the synagogue but he also began to spread the good news in a more zealous way elsewhere in Corinth. While doing that, however, he met opposition from the Jews because they opposed the gospel of Jesus Christ and hence they spoke injuriously against Christ. Paul therefore told them that since they refused to accept Christ their Messiah-Savior, he would go with the gospel to the Gentiles. So he ended up at the house of Justus—which was right next door to the synagogue—and continued to preach the good news of Jesus Christ. Even the ruler of the synagogue, Crispus, and his whole family came to the Lord; but mostly the converts to Christ were Gentiles.

Shortly thereafter fierce opposition arose, resulting in Paul evidently becoming somewhat hesitant as to whether he should stay in Corinth. He had previously been driven out of city after city, and consequently he was wondering whether he should stay or leave. That very night the Lord appeared to him in a vision and said: "Paul, remain here and do not be silent. I am with you. No one can set his hand upon you for I have many people in this city." When Paul heard this word in the vision, he stayed in Corinth a year and six months. After Gallio became Achaia's proconsul, the Jews unitedly brought Paul into the court of Gallio and accused him. Gallio in response said that since their complaint involved matters pertaining to their religious law, he would not be a judge over such questions. Afterward, Paul still stayed for some further time in Corinth. So that was how the church in Corinth began.

The People Who Comprised the Church in Corinth

Since Jews indeed ask for signs, and Greeks seek wisdom; but we preach Christ crucified, to Jews an offence, and to nations foolishness; but to those that are called, both Jews and Greeks, Christ God's power and God's wisdom. Because the foolishness of God is wiser than men, and the weakness of God is stronger

> than men. For consider your calling, brethren, that there are not many wise according to flesh, not many powerful, not many high-born. But God has chosen the foolish things of the world, that he may put to shame the wise; and God has chosen the weak things of the world, that he may put to shame the strong things; and the ignoble things of the world, and the despised, has God chosen, and things that are not, that he may annul the things that are; so that no flesh should boast before God (I Corinthians 1:22-29).

From this bible passage we realize that those believers in the church in Corinth were mostly common people—not wise but foolish, not of high position but low, not powerful but weak. In short, most of them were nobodies. But though they were nobodies, Paul went on to describe what some of them had been, with these words:

> Do ye not know that unrighteous persons shall not inherit the kingdom of God? Do not err: neither fornicators, nor idolaters, nor adulterers, nor those who make women of themselves, nor who abuse themselves with men, nor thieves, nor covetous, nor drunkards, nor abusive persons, nor the rapacious, shall inherit the kingdom of God. And these things were some of you; but ye have been washed, but ye have been sanctified, but ye have been justified in the name of the Lord Jesus, and by the Spirit of our God (6:9-11).

Some of these nobodies were quite notorious sinners; yet, by the grace of God, when the gospel was preached to these people, they were washed, sanctified, and justified in the name of the Lord Jesus and by the Spirit of God. So when Paul wrote this first letter to the Corinthians, he addressed them as having been sanctified in Christ Jesus—called saints. Think of that! They were nobodies, even a notorious, sinful people with a wicked lifestyle; but when the gospel of Jesus Christ and Him crucified was preached to them, what grace came upon them! They were sanctified, that is to say, they were set apart from the world. They were also justified. They were even called saints; not called *to be* saints, but they then and there were called saints. They had been sinners before but now they were saints, separated from the world to God. That was the power of Jesus Christ and Him crucified.

Not only that, but when Paul continued to preach Jesus Christ and Him crucified to them, we learn from this same letter of Paul's that these people were enriched in Christ Jesus, they having become rich in the word of God, in all knowledge, and were not behind anybody in spiritual gifts (1:5-7a). They had a very promising beginning, and Paul had held out great hope for them; for he further wrote concerning these Corinthian believers that they were "awaiting the revelation of our Lord Jesus Christ: who shall also confirm you to the end, unimpeachable in the day of our Lord Jesus Christ"—such was Paul's great hope for them who "[had] been called into the fellowship of [God's] Son, Jesus Christ [the] Lord" (1:7b-9).

Our Calling:
Sharing in the Fellowship of God's Son

Here we have been told that we are all called. But into what have we been called? Paul tells us that we all have been called into a fellowship—into a sharing together of the fellowship of God's Son, Jesus Christ the Lord. Think of that! In this universe of ours there is a fellowship that is different from all other fellowships in the world: it is the divine fellowship of the Father and the Son in the Spirit. God's Son, Jesus Christ, has a fellowship with His Father, the two of Them sharing everything together in the Spirit in love, in perfect harmony, in one mind, in one purpose. It is the closest most intimate and sweetest fellowship in the entire universe; and God called the Corinthians to join Him in that fellowship.

God has likewise called us to join in, but this fellowship can only be joined through new birth. You must be born into that fellowship; you must receive the life of God in order to be in that fellowship. The Son will share with us everything that He has with the Father; or to put it in an even more striking way: the Son will share His Father with us, and the Father will share His Son with us, thus making it such a rich, glorious and wonderful fellowship into which we have been called.

Think of that! We once belonged to the world—in nature: wicked, perverse, corrupt, fading—and now we are called out of that dissolute world into the fellowship of God's Son. We can share the Father with God's Son and vice versa. Think of that! This is the calling all we Christians possess in common. Moreover, as Paul declared: "God is faithful" and has sufficient grace to enable us to fulfill that calling. Paul held out great hope for the Corinthian believers—those sinners who became saints; and Paul expected them to truly live a saintly life to the glory of God. Indeed, from his perspective, everything is possible with God.

Years Later:
Paul Learns of Church Problems at Corinth

Paul was with the Corinthian believers for a year and six months—quite a long time; and later on, Apollos arrived on the scene and taught them. So, actually, they were much blessed by God's provision of ministries of the word of God; and hence, they should have progressed very quickly towards maturity. But when Paul was in Ephesus on his third missionary journey (cf. I Corinthians 16:8), he heard bad news about them (I Corinthians 1:11), things which were contrary to what they had been called into. Also, some of the Corinthian believers had even written him asking for his counsel regarding some very serious church matters (I Corinthians 7:1). In response Paul wrote his I Corinthians epistle in about the year 57 A.D. from Ephesus. Actually, what we know of as I Corinthians was Paul's second letter to the Corinthians because a first letter had apparently been lost to us (I Corinthians 5:9). For the remainder of our time today I would like for us to consider together these various church problems at Corinth and how the apostle of Christ was used of God to address them.

Unity versus Division

Now because these Corinthian believers had been called into the fellowship of God's Son, therefore, they were all one in Christ Jesus since Christ is not divided (cf. I Corinthians 1:13a). So to fulfill their calling, they had to be one with one another. They had to have Christ as their center and none else. If people have Christ as the center and nothing and no one else, then they are centered upon Christ and they are automatically one. We believers can only be one by being one *in Christ*. So we learn from Paul's epistle that the first problem among the Corinthians was that instead of being centered upon Christ, they began to shift their center towards various servants of Christ. Some said, "I am of Paul; I am for Paul. He led me to Christ, so I am for him." Others said, "I am of Apollos. He taught me the word of God, so I am for him." And others said, "I am of Cephas (i.e., the apostle Peter) because he is more original time-wise; for Cephas was the first apostle." While still others said, "We are even better; for we are exclusively of Christ. You are not of Christ; but we are of Him" (I Corinthians 1:10-12). Thus, instead of being united, they were divided.

Though these brethren at Corinth were not yet separated, for they still met together, nevertheless there was much party spirit present. It was a violation of the very meaning of the

The Church in Corinth

fellowship into which they had been called. We are called into the fellowship of God's Son Jesus Christ. And though it is true that Paul sowed the seed and Apollos watered, these servants of God were nothing; for it was God who gave the increase (3:6-7). So these Corinthian believers in Christ should have centered themselves upon Christ and Christ alone and should not have focused their eyes upon men because they were simply God's ministering servants (3:5). Paul in essence was saying here as follows: "You actually make yourself too small. You think: 'I am of Paul; Paul is enough for me.'" "No," Paul said, "Paul, Apollos, Cephas, even life and death, all things are yours; and you are Christ's, and Christ is God's" (see 3:21-23).

So the first problem with the life in the church at Corinth was that somehow they had shifted their attention and focus from Christ to the servants of Christ, from God to men; and because of this deviation, there were divisions among them. What a serious problem this was! Paul therefore dealt with this case first. This was not something they had written to him and asked about; rather, it was something he had heard from the household of Chloe (1:11), and he felt it was the most serious of all the problems facing the Corinthian Church.

We who are called into the fellowship of God's Son—can we be divided? We are one in Christ. There is "the unity of the Spirit" that has been given to us and we must diligently keep that unity (Ephesians 4:3). We must receive everyone whom Christ has received (Romans 15:7); for all those who believe on the Lord Jesus are brothers and sisters in the body of Christ and are therefore in the same fellowship. We are all sharing Christ Jesus and we should never shift our attention away from Him to anything or anyone else, not even to the greatest men of God, because that will adversely affect our unity in Christ Jesus. Hence we learn from I Corinthians 1-4 that that was the first and major problem in the church at Corinth—unity versus division.

Holiness versus Worldliness

A second problem is to be found in Paul's letter, chapters 5 and 6, and it can be defined as holiness versus worldliness. We who believe in Christ are called saints; all the Corinthians were called saints, thus meaning that they were separated from the world. Their behavior, their conduct, their life should be different from the world's. Unfortunately, though the Corinthian believers were justified by the grace of God in their having been saved, and though they had the new life of Christ in them, they were still living in the old way. They had continued to sin just as the world was doing, but they did so in even a worse manner than the world (5:1). Moreover, they were defrauding one another and bringing lawsuits against one another into the Gentile—that is, into the worldly—courts (6:1, 6). In other words, there was no separation from the world. They should have been holy because God is holy, and we His people must therefore be holy. And holy means "separated unto God."

In this section of his epistle Paul is found employing some familiar typological terms from the Old Testament to underscore the need for holy living on the part of the Corinthian believers. He wrote (in 5:6b-8) that we Christians have had the Lord Jesus as our Paschal or Passover Lamb and we are now to live in the reality of the Feast of Unleavened Bread that in the Old Testament times had continued on for seven more days following the Passover Feast, seven days signifying a complete circle of time (cf. Exodus 12:1-28, 13:1-10). By which Paul here meant that once having eaten the Paschal Lamb—which is to say that after having believed in Jesus as our sin offering—we are to keep the Feast of Unleavened Bread throughout the rest of our lives. We should not have any leaven—not even a crumb of it (cf. Exodus 12:15-20) upon us (leaven referring typically, of course, to sin or any kind of moral or doctrinal corruption). The Corinthian believers were living, as it were, in the time of the Feast of Unleavened Bread and were therefore supposed to be living a holy life separated from the world, but they were not doing so.

The people of the world may take each other to court, those of the world may defraud each other, and commit sins of every kind; but this is not the way we Christians are supposed to live and conduct ourselves. Yet this was what the Corinthian believers were doing, and hence, they were no different from the unbelieving world and were even worse than the world. Thus it could be said that holiness versus worldliness posed a second serious problem for these believers in the church at Corinth.

Discipline versus Indulgence

From reading chapters 7 to 10 of I Corinthians we can discern that a further problem which had emerged among the Christians at Corinth had to do with discipline versus indulgence. As God's people we ought to be those who are disciplined. We are disciples of the Lord Jesus, and as His disciples we need to be willing to receive discipline from the Lord. One of the works of the Holy Spirit is to discipline us, and we ourselves should cooperate in that work of self-discipline; that is what we should experience in our lives continually. Instead of that being the case, however, the Corinthian believers indulged themselves in several respects. For instance, they were not disciplined in the matter of married life, and so they had questions concerning marriage. They also had questions with regard to the matter of eating and drinking—such as whether they could buy and consume meat which had been offered to the idols. The idol-worshiping priests would sell the meat, and it was usually the best quality at the cheapest price in the market. So the question which arose was whether believers could buy this meat and eat it. Furthermore, during those days the social times and feasts were held within the idol-temple area, and so they had questioned whether they would be correct in going to the temple and having a social time.

Some believers had expressed their opinion as follows: "We have spiritual knowledge that idols are nothing, for we have only one God. Therefore, going to the temple or eating things which have been offered to idols: all that is nothing." They had reasoned in this manner because in reality they liked to feast and have a friendly social time with the world. And by reasoning that since they had the knowledge of the truth, they felt they had the freedom to indulge in such activities. Instead, these indulgent believers should have had love and concern in their hearts for those brethren in their midst with weak consciences who, upon observing what they—with their greater knowledge and freedom—were doing, might fall into sin by doing the same things. And thus these more knowledgeable believers had ended up sinning themselves in their having wounded the weak consciences of those other believers and in having thus also sinned against Christ.

Instead of being a disciplined people, some of the church brethren in Corinth had indulged their flesh by gratifying its desire to enjoy what they deemed would be good social times with the world but which were actually questionable. Such was the description of certain aspects of church life in Corinth at that time, as was revealed by the apostle Paul in his epistle.

Spiritual Order versus Carnal Freedom

A still further problem confronting the Corinthian church revolved around the issue of spiritual order versus carnal freedom. This problem we see addressed by the apostle in his letter's chapters 11 to 14. In the house of God there is an order. At the Lord's Table we need to examine ourselves before we take the loaf and the cup that we may not come to the Table unworthily and eat judgment upon ourselves. When the Lord Jesus had the first Lord's Table, it had occurred during the

Passover Feast; so in those early days, the Christians usually connected a love feast with the Lord's Table. They would have a love feast together and then have the Lord's Table. But what happened in Corinth was that those who were rich would come to the meeting place for the church's love feast and eat their good food and drink whereas those who were poor had nothing to eat and thus starved. Then, after that, the church would have the Lord's Table. So Paul counseled that such an arrangement was not honoring the Lord at all.

Later on, we find that the love feast and the Lord's Table were separated, for Paul wrote that he had "received from the Lord and now I deliver to you what had happened at the first Lord's Table." It was not the love feast that night which was commanded to be observed, but simply that the loaf and the cup were to be taken in remembrance of Him. If the love feast was a distraction from remembering the Lord, then it was better to separate the Lord's Table from the love feast.

But among these Corinthian believers there was fleshly freedom present: they felt free to do whatever they wanted instead of observing spiritual order. The same lack was true in the other meetings of the Corinthian church: there was no order in what took place. Many of the brethren did not like to keep their proper place in the church meetings. Paul therefore had to teach them that whatever they did during the meetings was for the purpose of edifying the church and that everything was to be done orderly and decently.

Faith and Obedience versus Unbelief and Insubjection

Chapters 15 and 16 of Paul's letter are concerned with faith and obedience versus unbelief and insubjection. Here the apostle is seen relating conduct with doctrine. If the conduct of the Corinthian believers was so loose as is described by Paul in his epistle, then they would quite naturally doubt even the doctrine of resurrection. Indeed, if there is no resurrection, as they themselves claimed, then people can eat and drink abundantly, for tomorrow they die, and that would be it. But if there *is* resurrection, then the evil conduct of these Corinthian Christians would become a problem for them. So we find here in Paul's writing that for the Christian, teaching and one's conduct cannot be separated. Among these Corinthian believers some did indeed doubt the resurrection. In response Paul declared that if there is no resurrection, then Christ is not resurrected; and if Christ is not resurrected, then we who believe in Him are the most hopeless and miserable of all people. But thank God there *is* resurrection! Christ is risen, and one day we will all be raised and will receive our reward. So taught the apostle Paul here.

The Corinthians Did Not Accept the Sanctifying Aspect of the Cross

In the life of the church at Corinth there was no testimony. Why was this so? Had not Paul preached to them determining to know nothing but Jesus Christ and Him crucified? Yes, he had. And had they not heard? They most certainly *had* heard, but sad to say, they had only received a part of the teaching of the cross: they had only received the *atoning* aspect of it and had rejected the *sanctifying* aspect of the cross. These Corinthians knew they were sinners and were afraid of going to hell, so they repented and believed in the Lord Jesus, and thus they were saved; but they still wanted to live according to the way of their old lives, they still wanted to live in the flesh and not grow up in Christ. So they remained as babes in Christ (I Corinthians 3:1) and became carnal Christians. Though they had the resurrection life of Christ in them, they still lived by their old life and continued to do the old things. Which meant that they did not receive the sanctifying aspect of the cross.

The Church in Corinth

The Lord Jesus took our sins away; He bore our sins in His body, so that when we believe in Him, His blood cleanses us from all our sin. Not only that, when the Lord was crucified on the cross, He took our old man; He took all of us with Him; our old man was crucified with Him on the cross—thus signifying that when Christ died, our old man died with Him as well; our flesh was crucified on the cross. The Corinthian believers, however, did not accept that aspect of the work of the cross. They only wished to receive its atoning aspect and rejected its sanctifying aspect.

What they needed was to experience more of the cross by allowing it to really work in their lives. They believed in the objective cross, the cross that was on Calvary's hill two thousand years ago; but they did not receive experientially the subjective aspect of the cross. Because of this, they could not live out Christ in a practical way; instead, they lived out the life of their old man, and it was a disgrace to the Lord.

Hence, what we need to learn from the church in Corinth is that we have a new life in us, and that the finished work of Christ is so complete. We need to accept all the finished work of Christ which He accomplished on the cross—not only that which concerns our sins but also what concerns our selves. We should consider ourselves as already dead in Christ Jesus and believe that when Christ was raised from the dead, we were raised with Him. So that today, it is no longer we who live, it is Christ who lives in us (Galatians 2:20a). We need to accept the cross and allow it to work in our lives in cutting off the deeds of the flesh and allowing Christ to live out His life through us. That is the only way we can fulfill our high calling, the only way we can live as Christ lived when He was on this earth. And such is the will of God. He wants to live through us corporately as Jesus Christ had lived on this earth two thousand years ago.

When Paul wrote what we know today as II Corinthians, he mentioned that it would be the third time he would be coming to the church in Corinth (12:14a, 13:1a). When was the second time he went there? It was not recorded in the book of Acts; but evidently Paul—after sending this so-called II Corinthian letter—did make a hurried trip to Corinth for the purpose of trying to help them out (cf. II Corinthians 2:1, 12:14, 13:1-2), but he was rejected (13:2-3a). After he was rejected, evidently he wrote another letter that was not II Corinthians. It was a very strong letter, written with many tears, and he asked Titus to take that letter to the Corinthian believers for the purpose of again trying to help them out (II Corinthians 2:4 with ch. 7:5ff.).

Godly Sorrow and Repentance

In II Corinthians he mentioned that he had an arrangement with Titus that they would meet in Troas, but Titus did not show up (2:12-13a). Paul was so disturbed and anxious regarding the Corinthian situation that he could not even stay there (2:13b), and so he continued on to Macedonia until Titus came there and brought the good news (7:6ff.). That strong letter which Paul had written with many tears had a salutary effect on the Corinthian believers; for they really repented: they were sorrowful with a godly sorrow, and so they repented. The tide had turned and Paul was immensely comforted (7:7-10a).

Concluding Observations

In writing II Corinthians Paul ended the letter very differently from the way he had ended I Corinthians. In ending the latter letter, he had declared most strongly: "If anyone does not love the Lord Jesus, let him be Anathema Maranatha—that is, Let him be cursed, for the Lord is coming" (see 16:22). The verb love there is *phileo* not *agapao* in the Greek original. In other words, if anyone has no good feelings, tender affection, or even kindness towards the Lord Jesus, that reflects the fact that that person could live in the indifferent and sinful way of the Corinthian believers and could disappoint Him in the way those Corinthians had grievously done. In so many words Paul

The Church in Corinth

was saying to the Corinthians: "You had been in a blessed position because of your conversion to Christ, but if now you do not even have good feelings towards the Lord Jesus, then you are accursed because the Lord is coming. It is that serious," said Paul. Even so, Paul's final words to his letter were these: "My love be with you all in Christ Jesus. Amen" (16:24). That noun-word love there is *agape*; the apostle thus meaning to say: "My Christian love—my love in Christ—towards you has not changed in the least."

Thank God that the conclusion to Paul's II Corinthian epistle is worded very differently. Wrote the now greatly-encouraged apostle: "For the rest, brethren, rejoice; be perfected; be encouraged; be of one mind; be at peace; and the God of love and peace shall be with you. ... The grace of the Lord Jesus Christ, and the love of God, and the communion of the Holy Spirit, be with you all" (13:11, 14). So we must thank God that by His grace and mercy the Corinthian believers had turned themselves around. They had finally accepted the much-needed sanctifying aspect of the cross in their lives.

In summing up in one word each of these two extant letters of Paul to the Corinthian church, we could use for I Corinthians the word carnality and for II Corinthians the word spirituality. It would appear on rather solid evidence that these heretofore unrepentant Corinthian believers were turned back to God, though there were still some there who did not repent (II Corinthians 12:21). But the church as a whole really did turn back. At the end of Paul's third missionary journey but before he went to Jerusalem for the last time, it is believed he actually spent three months in Corinth (cf. Acts 20:1-3a w/ Romans 16:1—Cenchrea being the eastern seaport of Corinth). If so, it was meant to demonstrate to the Corinthian believers that fellowship had been renewed with joy.

We can learn much from the life of the church in Corinth. What occurred there can serve as a warning to us. This church's history reflects the disappointing fact that the believers there had failed to receive in experience the sanctifying aspect of the cross. So how we need the cross to really work in each of our lives in order that our old man's fleshly deeds may be cut off and Christ may live through us; and then God's blessing will be upon us. May the grace of the Lord Jesus Christ, the love of God, and the communion of the Holy Spirit be with us all is my prayer.

Dear heavenly Father, we want to thank Thee for the high calling which Thou hast called us into, even into the fellowship of Thy Son, our Lord Jesus Christ. Lord, how holy that fellowship is, how glorious it is; and yet, Lord, we do acknowledge that oftentimes we disappoint Thee. Oftentimes we are not what we ought to be; we are not what Thou dost want us to be. Indeed, we do not allow Thee to live out Thy life through us. Instead, we stand in Thy way and bring disgrace to Thee. Lord, we do hate ourselves; we do come and tell Thee that we are now willing to deny ourselves, take up the cross, and follow Thee daily. Lord, we pray that Thou mayest get through to us so that Thou mayest live in and through us as a company of Your people to the praise of Thy glory. We ask in Thy name. Amen.

Chapter Nine

THE CHURCH IN EPHESUS

Acts 19:1-10—And it came to pass, while Apollos was at Corinth, Paul, having passed through the upper districts, came to Ephesus, and finding certain disciples, he said to them, Did ye receive the Holy Spirit when ye had believed? And they said to him, We did not even hear if the Holy Spirit was come. And he said, To what then were ye baptised? And they said, To the baptism of John. And Paul said, John indeed baptised with the baptism of repentance, saying to the people that they should believe on him that was coming after him, that is, on Jesus. And when they heard that, they were baptised to the name of the Lord Jesus. And Paul having laid his hands on them, the Holy Spirit came upon them, and they spoke with tongues and prophesied. And all the men were about twelve. And entering into the synagogue, he spoke boldly during three months, reasoning and persuading the things concerning the kingdom of God. But when some were hardened and disbelieved, speaking evil of the way before the multitude, he left them and separated the disciples, reasoning daily in the school of Tyrannus. And this took place for two years, so that all that inhabited Asia heard the word of the Lord, both Jews and Greeks.

Acts 20:17-35—But from Miletus having sent to Ephesus, he called over to him the elders of the [church]. And when they were come to him, he said to them, Ye know how I was with you all the time from the first day that I arrived in Asia, serving the Lord with all lowliness, and tears, and temptations, which happened to me through the plots of the Jews; how I held back nothing of what is profitable, so as not to announce it to you, and to teach you publicly and in every house, testifying to both Jews and Greeks repentance towards God, and faith towards our Lord Jesus Christ. And now, behold, bound in my spirit I go to Jerusalem, not knowing what things shall happen to me in it; only that the Holy Spirit testifies to me in every city, saying that bonds and tribulations await me. But I make no account of my life as dear to myself, so that I finish my course, and the ministry which I have received of the Lord Jesus, to testify the glad tidings of the grace of God. And now, behold, I know that ye all, among whom I have gone about preaching the kingdom of God, shall see my face no more. Wherefore I witness to you this day, that I am clean from the blood of all, for I have not shrunk from announcing to you all the counsel of God. Take heed therefore to yourselves, and to all the flock, wherein the Holy Spirit has set you as overseers, to shepherd the [church] of God, which he has purchased with the blood of his own. For I know this, that there will come in amongst you after my departure grievous wolves, not sparing the flock; and from among your own selves shall rise up men speaking perverted things to draw away the disciples after them. Wherefore watch, remembering that for three years, night and day, I ceased not admonishing each one of you with tears. And now I commit you to God, and to the word

of his grace, which is able to build you up and give to you an inheritance among all the sanctified. I have coveted the silver or gold or clothing of no one. Yourselves know that these hands have ministered to my wants, and to those who were with me. I have shewed you all things, that thus labouring we ought to come in aid of the weak, and to remember the words of the Lord Jesus, that he himself said, It is more blessed to give than to receive.

Ephesus: Another New Move of the Holy Spirit

It will be recalled from an earlier message in this series that the Holy Spirit felt it necessary to make a new move from Jerusalem to Antioch of Syria. And we shall learn in today's message how the Holy Spirit would make another new move, which would now take place in the important Asia Minor city of Ephesus. As was made clear previously the church in Jerusalem had been too much tied up with Judaism, and the church in Syrian Antioch was mainly composed of Gentiles. But the church in Ephesus was composed of both Jews and Gentiles, and God made them "one new man" (see Ephesians 2:11-15). So in Ephesus, we find another move of the Holy Spirit.

It will also be recalled that during the second missionary journey of the apostle Paul and after having gone through the Galatian countries, he was actually purposing to go to Asia Minor because at that time it was a highly populated Roman province. Nevertheless, though Paul had the idea of going there to preach the word of God, he was forbidden by the Holy Spirit from doing so (see again Acts 16:6). Unable to understand, we would think that because the province of Asia was close by, it would be the natural place for God's servant to go to next. It being a very populous place, it was quite reasonable to think that they too should hear the gospel of Jesus Christ. That is our human reasoning and human strategy at work. But the Holy Spirit forbade Paul to go to Asia Minor because He had something else in mind. Thank God, Paul and his companions were sensitive and obedient to the Holy Spirit. And thus He was able to lead them into Europe, with the result being that the gospel crossed over the Aegean Sea from the Asian continent into the continent of Europe.

On the way back to Antioch during the latter period of his second missionary journey Paul went to Ephesus, but he spent just one Sabbath there (Acts 18:19ff.). On that Sabbath he went into the synagogue and preached the word of God. Evidently the Holy Spirit was working, for after Paul finished preaching, people there asked him to stay on. However, he told them that he felt urged to go to Jerusalem, but he promised them that if the Lord willed, he would come back to them (Acts 18:20-21).

Nevertheless, Paul left Aquila and Priscilla behind at Ephesus (Acts 18:19a). We may recall that when he was in Corinth he had stayed with Aquila and Priscilla because they were of the same trade as his, which was tent-making. It so happened that when Paul had left Europe, he came back to Asia with Aquila and Priscilla (Acts 18:18a); but when he departed Ephesus, he left this couple behind. That was an example of the wonderful strategy of God, for during the period when these two were in Ephesus, a man came from Alexandria in Egypt whose name was Apollos. He was very eloquent, well acquainted with the Scriptures, and knew the way of the Lord up to a point; but he only knew the baptism of John. Which meant that Apollos knew repentance and that he should believe on the One who was coming; but that was all he knew related to salvation, and so he came to Ephesus and boldly proclaimed the word of God in the synagogue.

As Aquila and Priscilla listened to this mighty preacher, they sensed there was something missing. So they took Apollos home and instructed him more exactly in the way of the Lord and salvation. The Scriptures tell us that Apollos subsequently had the idea of going to Achaia and more specifically to Corinth, and the Ephesian brethren therefore wrote a letter of recommendation on his behalf.

By this fact we thus come to know that in Ephesus there were already brethren there besides Aquila and Priscilla. Most likely, therefore, and though Paul had preached there but once, the Lord had nonetheless won some to himself. During Aquila and Priscilla's stay there the Lord continued to work, and the church in Ephesus met first in the house of Aquila and Priscilla (cf. I Corinthians 16:19b).

"Did You Receive the Holy Spirit When You Believed?"

On his third missionary journey Paul went again to Ephesus, which became the center of his ministry in the province of Asia Minor. Upon arriving there he found twelve disciples; but as he talked with them Paul sensed that there was something amiss. These men were indeed disciples, yet during their conversation he discovered that there was something not quite right. So he asked them a question: "Did you receive the Holy Spirit when you believed?"

And they said, "Well, we do not even know if the Holy Spirit has come."

So Paul inquired of them, "What baptism have you received?"

They replied: "We received the baptism of John."

So Paul explained to these men the following: "This that you received is the baptism of repentance, telling people to believe in the One who would come afterward, and that is Jesus."

Paul therefore began to share with them that Messiah Jesus had already come and told them what the Lord had done on the cross. The whole plan of salvation was opened up to those twelve, and they readily believed and were baptized in the name of the Lord Jesus—the believer's baptism.

Those twelve disciples of John the Baptist had believed, but their faith was objective in nature; for they had believed that their Messiah would be coming and that when the Messiah finally came, He would redeem them. They had that objective knowledge but they lacked a personal relationship with the Lord Jesus. They had heard about the Lord Jesus but they did not know Him as their personal Savior. They did not have that subjective experience of the Lord.

Today we find that there are many people like this in Christianity who profess that they are Christians, that they believe; yet they do not have a living relationship with the Lord Jesus. That living relationship comes only through the Holy Spirit because it is He who gives our spirit a new birth. He it is who reveals Christ Jesus in us. It is the Holy Spirit who dwells in us, and by His indwelling, the Lord Jesus dwells in us. We have a living relationship with the Lord himself. Hence, how important it is that we have such a relationship with Him. Thank God for those twelve disciples of John the Baptist. We do not know whether they were disciples of John before Apollos came or whether they became disciples of John through Apollos but before Apollos himself knew better. Nevertheless, those twelve were added to the church in Ephesus.

The Separation of Christianity from Judaism

After that, Paul went to the synagogue every Sabbath for three months. He reasoned and persuaded them about the things concerning the kingdom of God. This was very unusual, because usually Paul would go to the synagogue a few times and then he would be cast out. But he was able to attend the synagogue in Ephesus for three whole months and presented the word of God. At the end of this period the Jews began to speak evil of the Way. At the very beginning of the Christian faith people had usually referred to those who believed in the Lord Jesus as people of the Way because they followed a way of life which was completely different from any other way of life on earth. It was different from the way of life of the Jews, from the way of life of the Gentiles, from the way of life of any nation. It was the Christian way, and so from the beginning, those who were believers were called the people of the Way. When some of the Jews in Ephesus began to speak evil of the Way, Paul left the synagogue and separated the disciples from the unbelieving Jews. It was a clear separation.

At the beginning of the Christian way—whether in Jerusalem or in other places where the Jews believed in the Lord Jesus—believers still went to the synagogue on the Sabbath; and they probably would also meet together on the first day of the week—on what we today call the Lord's day—to remember the resurrection of Jesus. So these believers would go to the synagogue not only on the Sabbath but even during the time of prayer. In Jerusalem, for example, they went to the temple during the time of prayer. Hence, from all this we can discern that there was not that clear a separation of Christianity from Judaism; in Ephesus, however, that separation ultimately came: Paul separated the disciples and began to meet separately instead of going back to the synagogue. As far as we can gather, the church must have begun meeting at that time in the house of Aquila and Priscilla (cf. I Corinthians 16:19b), but so far as the work of Paul was concerned, he at this time of separation commenced using the school of Tyrannus as the place for preaching the word of God. This went on in that manner for a period of two years.

To the best of our knowledge there were five gymnasiums in Ephesus at that time, and these were places where people would go after their day's work for recreation and for listening to lectures on different subjects of interest. We are told (I do not know how accurate it is) that from 11:00 a.m. to 4:00 p.m. was the leisure time for the people in Ephesus, and usually they would go to these gymnasiums for the aforementioned purposes during that time every day. Thus for two years Paul lectured in the school of Tyrannus daily. Today, by contrast, we find that our Christian meetings are too much. For instance, we here meet on Sunday, on Wednesday, and every other Friday, and probably we feel it is a little too much. But Paul daily lectured in the school of Tyrannus for some two years. Not only that, we also know from the record in Acts that he was in Ephesus for three years altogether (20:31); and during those three years the apostle faithfully preached the word of God—in all lowliness and with tears and with trials "through the plots of the Jews" (20:19)—and did so not only in public but also privately in their homes (20:20b). Moreover, Paul did not withhold anything from them that would be profitable to them (20:20a). As Paul himself said, he preached to the people in Ephesus "the whole counsel of God" (cf. 20:27). No wonder the work of the Holy Spirit was most evident in Ephesus.

During those same three years Paul not only preached the word of God, he also worked as a tent-maker. He said to the Ephesian church elders: "Behold my hands. These two hands have supplied the needs for myself and for my fellow workers during this period of time" (20:34). Some Bible commentators have observed that having worked in such a way Paul's hands eventually became quite rough and tinted. This would thus explain why he would say, "Behold my hands." Nevertheless, every day he would go to the school of Tyrannus and preach the word of God. Oh, how much the apostle Paul labored for the Lord through his faithful preaching and served as a positive example to all the believers there. So the church in Ephesus was greatly blessed by the Lord through His servant.

The Whole Counsel of God

Paul was in Corinth for a year and a half, but he told us in his I Corinthians epistle that he was not able to really share with

The Church in Ephesus

them the whole counsel of God (cf. 3:1-3a). There was nothing more precious and dear to the heart of the apostle Paul than the whole counsel of God—the mystery of God and of the Christ—that which God had revealed to him in such a special way. When he was in Corinth he was only able to share with them the Faith's basic fundamentals—Jesus Christ and Him crucified. He was not able to share with them the wisdom of God that was shrouded in mystery. It was all because the believers in the church at Corinth had remained babes, they not having grown up; and because they had remained babes, all which Paul could do was feed them with milk, for in such a state they could not digest solid food (3:1-3). But with the church in Ephesus, it was different: there were believers there with whom Paul was able to share the whole counsel of God, the eternal purpose of God, the mystery of God. He did not withhold anything from them (Acts 20:27). Now why was it so?

We know that the Corinthians were not less intelligent than the Ephesians. They were probably even more intelligent, yet Paul was able to share with the Ephesian believers what he could not share with the Corinthian believers. The reason for this is not related to one's intelligence but to one's heart. The Ephesian believers had such love in their hearts for the Lord that Paul was able to share with them without restraint. On the other hand, though the Corinthian believers were highly intelligent, their hearts were divided. They did not have a love for the Lord, and because of this, Paul was not able to share with them the whole counsel of God. So having an ability to know the full purpose of God in a real way is not a matter of how intelligent we are; it is a matter of what the condition of our heart is. If we love the Lord with our whole heart, the Lord will share with us His whole heart. Otherwise, we may know the Lord, but our knowledge of Him will be incomplete and highly limited.

Two Noteworthy Traits of the Ephesian Church—God's Word and Love

When Paul wrote I Corinthians, he ended it by saying: "If anyone does not love the Lord, let him be accursed. The Lord is coming." But when he ended his letter to the Ephesians, he wrote: "May grace be unto all who love the Lord with undying love." What a great difference!

There were two outstanding traits in the church in Ephesus; one was the word of God and the other was love. God's word was preached faithfully and in the power of the Holy Spirit; and it was received into the hearts of the Ephesian believers. The word of God worked in them in such a way that they burned their books of magic. Ephesus at that time was a large, wealthy, commercial city. It was also famous for its idolatrous temple. We are told that the temple in Ephesus was deemed to be one of the seven wonders of the ancient world. It required 120 years to construct that temple, and it became a place of immorality. Yet God's word worked there in such power. The people who believed in the Lord had all previously delved in the occult, in magic, and in spiritism; but when they believed in the Lord Jesus, the word of God worked in their hearts to such a degree that they brought out their magic books and burned them—fifty thousand silver pieces' worth. The word of God was powerful in their midst, and there was love in the hearts of the believers. That was the kind of life which marked the church in Ephesus at that time.

The Decline in the Ephesian Church

At a certain point Paul was imprisoned in Rome. When he was released from prison, he was able to travel again and revisit some of the old places. Most likely he also went to Spain during the few remaining years of his life after he was released (cf. Romans 15:24, 28).

The Church in Ephesus

Paul also went to Ephesus. His stay there this time was very short, but he was there long enough for him to have realized that the situation had changed. When he wrote the Letter to the Ephesians from his Roman prison, which probably occurred in 62 or 63 A.D., he was able to share with them most fully. The word was full and they loved the Lord with undying love. He was still able to share with them the whole counsel of God—indeed, the mystery of Christ—because the love among the Ephesian brethren was still there. But after Paul was released from his Roman imprisonment and came again to Ephesus for the above-mentioned short visit, he discovered the condition of the brethren had changed. In fact, it had become exactly as he had prophesied to the elders would happen when he spoke to them in Miletus at the conclusion of his third and final missionary journey (Acts 20:15-35).

On that occasion Paul had bypassed Ephesus; but being close by in Miletus, he called the elders of the church in Ephesus to come to Miletus, where he shared with them his last words. The apostle told them how he had labored in their midst and that he would not be able to see them anymore. He exhorted them to watch the flock because he said there would be people coming in like wolves and they would bring in other doctrines. Even among the elders themselves, warned Paul, there would be people trying to teach things that would draw them away from Christ to themselves. Sure enough, after Paul was released and he revisited them, he found something was different. Most likely the first group of elders who had been raised up by God in the Ephesian church had passed away; so when Paul went back again to Ephesus after his release from his Roman imprisonment, he found that the situation there had changed.

This we learn from the first chapter of I Timothy, for Timothy had been urged—even begged—by Paul to remain in Ephesus (1:3a) to where Paul's younger co-worker had been left behind by the apostle earlier. So from I Timothy's opening verses we are made aware of what had happened among the brethren in the Ephesian church. First of all, they had not kept strictly to the word of God. Instead, there were people teaching other doctrines, things that would not contribute to the Faith. Indeed, they had deviated from love, which is the very purpose of the word of God. His word should create love, but instead of that being true among the brethren they began to talk about fables, myths, and genealogies. Moreover, the Judaistic influence had begun to come in, and some began to teach the law. So when there on his short visit Paul discovered that other doctrines and other teachings had come in to squeeze out the truth of the word of the Lord; and when such things happen, usually love will begin to grow cold. God's word and love cannot be separated. Where there is truth, it should produce love; where there is love, people will love the truth; but when the truth begins to be diluted, then the love which had been present begins to grow cold. That was the situation in the church at Ephesus which Paul had observed and sensed while on his visit following his release from his first Roman imprisonment.

Usually, the trait that is the strongest in a person or in a church will be the very concentrated target of the Enemy. Oftentimes in history it is that in which the church is strongest that it falls; and that is the result of the clever work of the Enemy. And in the church at Ephesus the strongest points, as we have seen, were the solid and full word of God and the love of the brethren for the Lord and for one another. It was on these two noteworthy traits of the Ephesian church which became the concentrated target of the Enemy. He drew the brethren away from the word of God into devoting themselves to genealogies, traditions, the law, other doctrines, philosophies, and speculations of every kind; and at the same time their love began to grow cold. All this is what is made known to us by Paul in his pastoral epistle of I Timothy.

In 64 A.D. the Roman Emperor Nero burned the city of Rome and accused the Christians of the crime, thus using the Christians as the scapegoats. Hence, from that moment onward

The Church in Ephesus

great persecution arose against the Christians, not only in Rome but also it began to spread elsewhere in the Empire. The apostle Paul was arrested a second time and sent back to Rome. Probably it was in 67 or 68 A.D. that Paul was martyred, but before he died he wrote his last letter to Timothy, his beloved son in the faith. At that time Timothy was in Ephesus again and Paul mentioned that all in Asia Minor had forsaken him (1:15). Now it was in that Roman province which was the area where Paul had spent three years of ministry, yet during this apostle's last days all believers in Asia had left him. There were exceptions, of course, and Timothy was one of them. Also, we learn from II Timothy that Aquila and Priscilla had meanwhile moved back from Rome to Ephesus, so they too were in Ephesus once again (cf. 4:19). Probably during that period there was a small group of people who were still standing for the testimony of God as well. But all this was the meager extent to these exceptions.

Now in II Timothy Paul wrote that the church is like a big house wherein there are vessels of honor and vessels of dishonor: some gold and silver vessels and some made of mud, clay, and wood. He who separates and purifies himself from the dishonored vessels shall be deemed a vessel of honor fit for the Master's use (2:20-21). Paul mentioned also in his epistle about seeking the Lord with those who call on the Lord with a pure heart (2:22). Evidently, therefore, when the church in Ephesus began to decline, there was still a small group of saints there who were standing for the Lord; and, of course, Timothy was in their midst. So Paul encouraged Timothy to be courageous and stand firm for the testimony of the Lord and not be afraid but be willing to suffer for the Lord's sake. That was the situation in Ephesus at that particular phase of the Neronian persecution.

We do not know anything further about the situation in the church at Ephesus until some thirty years later. From tradition we surmise that after Paul was martyred (in about 67 or 68

A.D.) the apostle John probably moved into Asia Minor and began to work there. Then, during the reign of Emperor Domitian he was exiled in 95 A.D. to the island of Patmos, which was a deserted island in the Aegean Sea. There was a mine there and most likely John was sent there to work in that mine. On one particular Lord's day, and as he was possibly gazing across the sea, he could perhaps even see the coastline of Asia, since Patmos was not that far away. He was most likely thinking of the churches there that he had served before he was banished, and it was on this occasion that he heard a voice behind him instructing him to write down what he would be seeing and hearing. That in fact would form the content of the book of Revelation, and it was probably written down in the year of his banishment.

Now in Revelation chapter 2 we learn that the risen Lord, through the apostle John, wrote a letter to the church in Ephesus. From this we therefore know that the church in Ephesus was still there; her lampstand was still there. Which means that the Ephesian believers seemed to have been able to continue on in their existence as a church. Now in His letter to that church the Lord wrote this: "I know thy works and thy labour, and thine endurance, and that thou canst not bear evil men; and thou has tried them who say that themselves are apostles and are not, and hast found them liars; and endurest, and hast borne for my name's sake, and hast not wearied ... Thou hatest the works of the Nicolaitanes, which I also hate" (vv.2-3, 6).

It seems as though these Christians were still keeping God's word, since it was through His word that they were able to discern the false teachers and the false apostles, and it was also God's word which told them to hate the Nicolaitans, that is to say, to hate the distinction which had developed between the clergy and laity. Evidently, therefore, those in the church at Ephesus appeared to be able to continue on with the word of God, but in a very different manner from what had been true of them decades earlier: the word of God was now being kept as a tradition instead of as a living faith. The believers still had the knowledge of God's word but without the word being the basis for a living faith: God's word was purely objective; it did not affect their life. So this was the situation in the church at Ephesus at this much later time. They still undertook many labors for the Lord, they still had much endurance, they even still had discernment through the word of God, and they rejected the laity-and-clergy distinction. In short, outwardly speaking the church in Ephesus had gone on well, but the risen Lord declared this: "I oppose you because you have left your first love."

By this time the church in Ephesus was most likely in the third generation already. In the first generation there had been revelation; the Holy Spirit had revealed Christ in them. Moreover, there had been the revelation of the whole counsel of God, and it was so powerful that these saints of God had truly not counted any cost in their devotion to the Lord Jesus. They had been willing to let everything go for the sake of the Lord. In the second generation, though, there appeared a gradual decline among them, as we find in Paul's I Timothy epistle. And in coming to the third generation we discover that God's word was being kept outwardly, perhaps even exactly and correctly; nevertheless, the life was no longer there. These believers were in such a disappointing condition that the Lord was impelled to say in exasperation to them: "Unless you repent and do the first works, I will remove your church lampstand" (see Revelation 2:5c).

How sad this was! Yet this condition of the church of God has happened in her history again and again. It is relatively easy to keep God's word as a tradition and be zealous for it and even fight for it. Yet such an attitude and action towards the word of God has not produced love in the heart. What the Lord is looking for is love. What is the use of much labor if there is no love behind it? Where there is no love God's truth will simply become a tradition. But where there is love you have living faith. What God requires of us is but one thing: love—that we may love Him with all our hearts and that we may love one another. That is the testimony which God is continually looking for in His people because "God is love" (I John 4:16b).

The church in Ephesus had fallen quite far (Revelation 2:5a). Outwardly they were correct, but inwardly they had fallen greatly, and so the Lord called for repentance (2:5b). I believe what the Lord is calling His people to do today is to repent. Time is a great form of testing. Oftentimes we Christians discover that we cannot endure the time. When we first believed in the Lord, when we were first constrained by His love, oh! How we loved Him with first love, with the best love; we loved Him with an undivided heart, with absolute obedience, and with no consideration for ourselves. But time began its work of testing upon us, and gradually either we were led away from God's word into other doctrines or we kept His word as merely a tradition and not as the basis of a living faith. Moreover, our love simultaneously began to fall away.

Is it not time that we wake up? Is it not time that we go before the Lord and repent? Where spiritually are we currently? Is the word of God still living in our midst? Can we say that we love Him and that we do not count the cost anymore? Or have we been counting what it will cost us if we repent and do resume loving the Lord, especially in these end-time last days? I am fearful that the condition of the church today is similar to what it was like with the Ephesian church back then, which in the latter case was under persecution. For them at Ephesus it was very costly, but if there is love, love can overcome for "love never fails" (I Corinthians 13:8a). So may our prayer for us today be: "Lord, restore our first love."

We know that after Domitian died, the apostle John was released, and evidently he went back to Ephesus. All we know today is gleaned from Church tradition which has asserted that John, who at near the end of the first century A.D. was quite old, would be carried into the church meeting by the younger brothers. The church brethren wanted to hear from him, so John said, "Little children, love one another." That was all he said. They then asked him if he had any more to say, and he said, "If you love one another, that is all that is necessary to be said." So we wonder whether through that apostle of love—whose ministry was that of recovery—the church in Ephesus was recovered, at least at that time. We do not know, but hopefully it was so.

What can we learn from the history of the church in Ephesus? I believe we have much to learn from that church, but especially in these two areas—the living word of God and His everlasting love.

Dear Lord, we want to thank Thee for giving us the story of the church in Ephesus. Lord, we thank Thee for her history. Thou dost encourage us, and Thou dost warn us. Lord, we pray that we may take heed to Thy word. Lord, do examine us, whether we have departed from the first love, and whether we are keeping Thy word not as a living revelation but merely as a tradition. Oh Lord, we do pray that Thou wilt restore us. We want to repent; we want to do the first works; we want to please Thee; we want Thee to be all and in all to us. We pray in Thy precious name. Amen.

Chapter Ten

THE CHURCH IN COLOSSAE

Acts 19:10—And this took place for two years, so that all that inhabited Asia heard the word of the Lord, both Jews and Greeks.

Colossians 2:6-10a—As therefore ye have received the Christ, Jesus the Lord, walk in him, rooted and built up in him, and assured in the faith, even as ye have been taught, abounding in it with thanksgiving. See that there be no one who shall lead you away as a prey through philosophy and vain deceit, according to the teaching of men, according to the elements of the world, and not according to Christ. For in him dwells all the fulness of the Godhead bodily; and ye are complete in him.

As we have been considering the life of the body of Christ as recounted in the book of Acts, we have presented the negative as well as the positive side of this body life. The negative side is comprised of the things we need to avoid and the positive side is comprised of the things we need to possess. As a matter of fact, the life of the body of Christ is one with the life of Christ himself because it is the same life and is therefore the one life. It is the life which the Lord Jesus lived out in His incarnated body, and this same life is now being lived out in His mystical body. Hence, whatever is contrary to, or different from, the life of Christ as lived out in His incarnated body cannot be deemed as being the life of the body of Christ on earth today. There is much we can learn from the life of the first-century churches because their life is the same which we have today. It is the very same life which Jesus lived out while on earth because the church is the body of Christ and its life is the life of Christ.

Now I would like for us today to consider together the life of the church in Colossae. It so happens that the name Colossae is not to be found anywhere in the book of Acts, but we do have a letter which was written by the apostle Paul to the church in Colossae. This town was one of the tri-cities situated in the Lycus Valley of Asia Minor. The other two communities were Laodicea and Hierapolis. In Paul's Letter to the Colossians the apostle mentioned Laodicea and Hierapolis (4:13) because these three cities together formed a tilted triangle of communities. They were close to each other, in fact within walking distance of each other, and in a sense they were all as one unit. Of these three communities, Laodicea, being a metropolitan city, was the most prominent one among them. Hierapolis was next in importance, and Colossae was viewed as the least of the three. And yet, to this little community's small church a great and highly important letter was written. How we thank God for this Letter to the Colossians! What would we be as Christians if we had not had this letter? Our knowledge and understanding of the Lord Jesus would not be full and complete. It is through this Letter to the Colossians that we can come to a full knowledge of Jesus.

The Birth of the Church in Colossae

As far as we know, before Paul wrote this letter he had never visited Colossae (see Colossians 2:1). In reading Paul's Letter to Philemon we do learn that he mentioned he would visit the brethren there (v.22). As it turned out, Paul's knowledge of the saints in Colossae had come from Epaphras, Philemon, and other people because he did not have a direct relationship with the church there.

The Church in Colossae

Now during the three years the apostle was in Ephesus, all in the province of Asia Minor, we are told in Acts, heard the word of the Lord (19:10). Because Ephesus was a capital city, the people in that Roman province would visit there. So during these three years Paul faithfully preached the word of the Lord to the people who came, and they all—both Jews and Gentiles—heard the word. It is for sure that Epaphras, who was from Colossae (Colossians 1:7-8, 4:12-13), was saved through the preaching of the apostle Paul. Philemon, also a native of Colossae, heard the gospel from Paul as well, and he and his whole family were saved (cf. Philemon 1-2, 10 with Colossians 4:9, 17). So through these brothers and sisters the church in Colossae had its beginning. Let us take a closer look at these choice saints in the Colossian church.

Epaphras

In his Letter to the Colossians Paul mentioned Epaphras and called him the beloved fellow bondman (1:7a). Now we know that the apostle Paul was himself a bondman of Jesus Christ (e.g., Romans 1:1a, Philippians 1:1a, Titus 1:1a), meaning he was a bondslave: he was a love slave of the Lord Jesus. He was one, as it were, who out of love had had his ear pierced for life (cf. Exodus 21:5-6). He belonged to the Lord Jesus. Paul was proud to call Epaphras the bondslave of Jesus Christ. After Epaphras believed in Jesus he became His bondslave; for he not only believed but he surrendered his whole life to the Lord. He too had had his ear pierced, as it were, and became a bondslave of Jesus Christ. But Paul also called him a faithful minister of Jesus Christ (1:7b). He was a faithful minister who ministered the word of God to the people in Colossae, in Laodicea, and in Hierapolis (cf. 1:2, 4:13).

Moreover, in the Letter to Philemon Paul called Epaphras "my fellow prisoner of Jesus Christ" (v.23). How had Epaphras become a prisoner in Rome? We do not know for sure; but one thing we can suppose is that he traveled almost a thousand miles from Colossae to Rome to find Paul in prison, and perhaps he was such a zealous person for the Lord in preaching the gospel there that he too was put in prison, where he became a fellow prisoner of Jesus Christ with the apostle Paul. Such was the person and character of Epaphras.

Philemon

In his Letter to Philemon Paul called him "the beloved and fellow workman" (v.16). Philemon was the beloved brother just as Paul had called Luke "the beloved physician" (Colossians 4:14). Philemon must have had a very gentle nature. He was a person of hospitality, and he expressed his faith and love in practical deeds. So all the saints received from him that gentleness and hospitality. He was also called Paul's fellow workman. We do not know what his profession was, but evidently, he was a well-to-do person because he had slaves. Onesimus was one of his slaves (Philemon 10, 16; Colossians 4:9a) who had robbed him (Philemon 18-19a) and fled away to Rome. In being a very hospitable person Philemon had opened his house for the church to meet there (Philemon 2b). Such was the character of this fellow workman of Paul's.

Apphia

Most likely Apphia (Philemon 2a) was the wife of Philemon. She was a dear sister, and if she had not been of one mind with her husband, it would have been very difficult for him to have opened their house for the church to meet there. As a matter of fact, for a family to open their house for such a purpose would probably mean that the wife would have the greater responsibility. So here we see that sister Apphia was of one mind with her husband and together they served the Lord, opening their home for the church to meet.

Archippus

Then there was Archippus. Paul called him my "fellow soldier" (Philemon 2b). Who was Archippus? Most likely he was the son of Philemon and Apphia (cf. Philemon 1-2). He was a young man who was a fellow soldier of the apostle Paul. As a young man he was fighting the good fight of faith. He was also in the ministry, serving the Lord (Colossians 4:17). So we see here a beautiful family, and the church in Colossae met in that home.

There was Epaphras, such a faithful minister; and with this beautiful family, we can imagine what the condition this little church meeting in that house was like. Indeed, in reading the Letter to the Colossians, we gain a glimpse of it. After Paul and Timothy heard of the Colossian church (since they had never been there), Paul wrote this: "We do not cease praying for you, after we have heard of your faith in Jesus Christ and the love which ye have towards all the saints, on account of the hope that you have reserved in heaven" (see Colossians 1:3-5).

We see in this little church the condition of the brothers and sisters there. They had faith in the Lord Jesus; they had love towards all the saints—no discriminating but having love for all the saints; and they had their hope in heaven and not upon this earth. We know these three elements are the chief ingredients of a Christian's walk. We will remember I Corinthians 13:13 that mentions faith, hope, and love. These are the three essential ingredients of one's Christian life and walk, and this little church had all three. Thus, we may say that this little church had a wonderful beginning. It was through the combined efforts of Epaphras, Philemon, Apphia and Archippus—through their life example and through their ministries—that a little church in Colossae was raised up. Most certainly it was a wonderful good beginning. Not many years hence, however, the condition of these saints would change for the worse.

Heresy Soon Comes In

It is believed that Paul was in Asia Minor between 54 and 58 A.D.; and when he wrote the Colossian letter it was in 62 or 63 A.D. Within that short a time, though, the condition in the Colossian church would undergo great change; for unfortunately, as is intimated in Paul's letter, some heresy had begun to come into the church. What happened? Some people had brought in some strange teaching, which commenced taking hold of the saints there and exerting a kind of evil influence upon them. What was the nature of that heresy? Well, there were actually two parts to it.

Heathen Gnosticism

Today we call what was a two-part aberration the Colossian heresy; for by carefully reading Paul's letter we discover that it was a strange combination of both heathen Gnosticism and Jewish ritualism. On the one hand, there was the coming into the church at Colossae of heathen Gnosticism, which served as the beginning of what later came to be known as Gnosticism as a philosophic movement. At a certain point in the history of the Colossian church there came into its midst a small group of people who claimed that they were those who knew—or had the access to the knowledge of—all things. They had a kind of secret wisdom which enabled them to understand the mystery of the universe. They could explain the creation. They believed in angels, and claimed to possess in themselves different levels of the manifestation of God. So on the one hand, it was gnostic philosophy, mysticism, and speculation all rolled up into one kind of teaching which began to come into the Colossian church.

Jewish Ritualism

On the other hand, there was this heresy's other aspect—that of Jewish ritualism. Under the influence of that small group of people who had come into their midst the Colossian saints began to observe days; moreover, some things these believers now could no longer touch and some things they could no longer eat; indeed, there were all kinds of Jewish rituals and ceremonies which they now had to observe. What a strange combination this heresy was! One would think that if you delved into all kinds of speculation and into metaphysics, philosophy, and mysticism, you would probably be an inhabitant of an ethereal realm as though floating somewhere in the air and would thus never come into contact with anything material or physical. How odd and bizarre, however, that this heretical teaching, which dwelt much on the metaphysical, nonetheless simultaneously called for the observance of Jewish ritualism that required contact with the physical and material world! How odd and bizarre, indeed; yet that was the Colossian heresy.

The Temptation of the Heresy

Why did this strange two-part heretical teaching have such a strong influence on that little church in Colossae? Probably for the following reason. After the saints in Colossae had heard the truth and had believed, they really grew well in the Lord. But in their desire to grow and mature even faster, they found that such unorthodox teaching nonetheless catered to the natural desire of man to do something. Like all of mankind everywhere they wanted to achieve something by their own efforts because that, in a sense, would feed their ego. So the propagators of this heresy came in, telling them that if they wanted to be perfect, if they wanted to be complete, if they wanted to have spiritual fullness, there was a way, and that way was through a combined sort of mysticism and ritualism. And that if they accepted this teaching and faithfully put it into practice, they would become spiritual faster and would enter into fullness. Needless to say, such teaching obviously appealed to the flesh of these Colossian believers, and it catered to their natural desires.

Let us be clear here that if people want to grow to fullness spiritually, it takes time. Naturally speaking, even physically, it takes time for a human's physical body to grow. So spiritually speaking, one must go through much pain and many trials, but gradually, that person will grow into maturity, into perfection, into completeness.

This heresy at Colossae was, wrote Paul, a teaching according to the elements of the world—according to man and not according to Christ (Colossians 2:8b). The purveyors of this heresy had entered into the midst of the Colossian believers claiming enticingly: "Yes, indeed, you can obtain a super knowledge; and if you follow our instructions, you shall be initiated immediately into the secret and shall be complete, perfect, and possess the fullness you seek after." This subtle heresy thus had to do with being initiated into certain secrets and observing certain ritualistic days and rules; and if all were faithfully followed, then a person would immediately enter into fullness. In fact, he or she would become spiritual almost instantly. Such teaching began to gain a grip on the Colossian saints and eventually exerted such an influence upon them that Epaphras, the faithful minister that he was (see again Colossians 1:7b), finding himself unable to cope with the situation, decided to take a distant and dangerous journey of almost a thousand miles to Rome to see Paul and seek out help from him.

In reading Paul's Letter to the Colossians one can readily see that when Paul heard what had happened in the church at Colossae he was really burdened for their situation. It may remind us of what the apostle had written in II Corinthians: "The care of the churches is upon me. Who is weak and I am

The Church in Colossae

not weak? Who is stumbled, and I burn not?" (see 11:28c-29) That was the heart of the apostle Paul. Such was the attitude and burden of Paul upon hearing of the unfortunate development in Colossae: his heart burned within him, impelling him to send a letter to the saints there. And in that letter he reveals to us why and how they had fallen into the trap of the Enemy and where the remedy lay.

The church in Colossae had a very solid foundation in its establishment. The believers there had faith; they also had hope; and they were filled with love. Nevertheless, a good beginning does not guarantee a good end, and such realization ought to serve as a warning to us. The Colossian church had been birthed with a good foundation, it having been well laid by all those faithful men and women mentioned earlier; yet the Enemy had come in and sowed the tares which had almost destroyed that church. God's Enemy not only perpetrated that evil act in the first century; he has continued to do so ever since, even in our own day. Let us not think, therefore, that because there is a good foundation there is no danger of saints being led astray. Brethren today must beware lest a similar development occur unbeknownst to them. The Enemy is continually trying to sow tares into the ground where wheat has been sown (Matthew 13:24-30).

As was pointed out earlier, with the Colossian believers it was not a case of carelessness, as though they did not care. They were not like the Corinthian believers, who were satisfied as long as they were assured of going to heaven; they had had no desire to grow in the Lord or to follow Him more closely. No, the Colossian believers were different: upon their believing in the Lord Jesus they had wanted to go onward with Him into fullness: they had wanted to become deeply spiritual. But in wanting to pursue after the Lord, these Colossian believers would have to deny themselves, take up their cross, and follow Him. They found, however, that that was difficult—like climbing a challenging mountain. Then came their way this subtle heretical teaching: "You don't need to go through all this; to the contrary, there is a way of wisdom which you can enter into quite easily which will enable you to know everything. Just observe a few rituals and follow a few rules and very soon you will be perfect, matured, and can enter into spiritual fullness." Such was the temptation which was held out to these Colossian saints as a shortcut to spirituality and to fullness.

Do any of us believe there are no such teachings today? Actually in Christianity currently there are many shortcuts being offered and they are not according to Christ but are according to the elements of the world and according to the teaching of men (Colossians 2:8) who claim that we can be spiritual instantaneously: "You do not need the cross nor need to pay any cost nor need to deny yourself. All you need to do is to hear and receive some wisdom, be initiated into its secrets, do a few things and keep away from certain other things, and you shall be perfect." How many people have fallen into the trap of such teaching! Today we are not completely free from such heretical teaching.

The Remedy to the Heresy

Why was it that the Colossian believers were so easily tempted and fell? It was due to the fact that though they had a good foundation they did not have a full knowledge of God's will; and because of that, they were easily tempted and soon led astray. Consequently, when Paul heard of their situation, he not only shared with them the full knowledge of God's will but he actually prayed for them along that very line. Indeed, Paul's Letter to the Colossians tells us how he prayed: "I pray that you may be filled with the full knowledge of God's will in all wisdom and spiritual understanding" (see 1:9b). *That* is what they needed. If church believers only have a good foundation, they are not protected from being led astray. We need to be filled with the full knowledge of God's will; that alone will keep us from being led astray.

A Full Knowledge of God's Will

What is the full knowledge of God's will? It is evident from the Colossian letter that Paul shared with the saints at Colossae the full knowledge of God's will (1:9-20). Such knowledge is centered upon His beloved Son, the Lord Jesus Christ. It is the supremacy of Christ; it is the preeminence of Christ; it is Christ who is all and in all (3:11b ASV). Paul told them that the Christ they knew is much greater than they realized. They thought they could have fullness outside of Christ; but there is no such thing because in the will of God all the fullness of the Godhead dwells in Him bodily, and anyone who believes in Christ is complete *in Him* (2:9-10). That is to say, it is the will of God to put everything of His wisdom and knowledge in His Son.

His Son is therefore the fullness of God's wisdom and knowledge. Everything is created in Christ, by Christ and for Christ (1:16); He is the beginning, He is the firstborn from the dead; He is the Head of the church; and it is through Him that all things are reconciled, gathered back and restored to God's original thought; through Him peace is made (1:18-20); all things are summed up in Christ Jesus (Ephesians 1:10b). Apart from Christ, there is no knowledge and no wisdom; apart from Him there is no fullness. Man can find everything in Christ; and outside of Him, all is vanity. Such is the full knowledge of God's will.

We need to know Christ in the will of God. What is the eternal purpose of God? What is the purpose that God has purposed and willed even before the foundation of the world? That purpose and will is Christ—He who is everything and in all. That is God's will. If we know this is God's will, then we will stay in Christ and not go astray.

Paul wrote: "After you have believed in the Lord Jesus, walk in Him, rooted and built up in Him. Do not be led astray by philosophy and vain deceit, according to the elements of this world, according to the teaching of men, and not according to Christ" (see Colossians 2:6-8). Everything must be according to Christ. Hence, we need to ask ourselves: Is what is being proclaimed as the way to perfection and fullness centered in Christ or will it draw us away from Christ? If, for instance, it is philosophy that is being put forward as the way to fullness, is it centered in Christ? If it is ritualism, is such focused on Christ? Or if it is mysticism, will that draw us to Christ or lead us away from Christ? Or if it is ceremonialism, will that uphold the centrality of Christ or lead us away from Christ? The matter at issue is, and ever shall be, Christ as the all and in all, for that is God's will for each and every one of us who believe because that, said Paul, is what he labored for (1:29a). For this Paul labored, to the end that he wished to present everyone completed and perfected in Christ Jesus (1:28b): "Christ in you, the hope of glory" (1:27b).

That prescription of Paul's for spiritual fullness is not only for us individual Christians, it is also for the whole church. It is Christ, who is all and in all. It is neither Jew nor Gentile, neither barbarian nor Scythian, neither the circumcised nor the uncircumcised, neither bondman nor freeman; but Christ is all, and in all (see 3:11 NASB). That is the full knowledge of God's will, and that is what we increasingly have to enter into in our Christian walk, both individually and collectively.

I thank God that He is exercising us these days to immerse ourselves in the Person and work of the Lord Jesus. We *think* we know His Person and work; and yes, we do know of it to some extent—that which is the foundation. Thank God for that good foundation, but we need to delve more deeply into the full knowledge of God's will. We need to know Christ as God knows Him, and that is infinite in its extent. There is so much more that we need to know; and in our knowing that this is

God's will, it will keep us away from the teaching of man and from the elements of this world.

Revelation of the Holy Spirit

How can we enter into the reality of such a full knowledge of God's will? May we see that it is more than that which other people can pass on to us. It is quite true, of course, that God has revealed the mystery to His apostles and prophets (cf. Ephesians 3:4b-5); and they have shared with us what God had revealed to them concerning the Lord Jesus. It came to them in revelation. God revealed His Son to them and He has been revealed; and today that full knowledge is an open secret. We can read of it in the word of God; but if we merely read it or merely hear it, we will not obtain and understand it. That is why Paul prayed for the Colossian believers. In his letter to them, in fact, and before he began to share with them what was on his heart, Paul prayed for them (1:9-10), because he knew that in sharing such revelation it would not become living unless the Spirit of God quickened the word to their hearts and minds.

Hence, when reading the word of God, we need to pray and ask Him to open our spiritual understanding; that not only will we have a mental apprehension or grasp of God's word, but that also the Holy Spirit will open up God's word and make it living and operative within us. That can only come by revelation of the Holy Spirit. We need to pray that God will open our spiritual understanding in order that His revelation is not only received mentally but that it also will be made real to us in our truly seeing Christ as all and in all and that outside of Him we need nothing else and seek for nothing else.

How much we need such prayer. It is only through prayer that light will come to us. Furthermore, besides prayer, we must have a willingness to be dealt with by God. Each time a further revelation of Jesus Christ comes to us, invariably it must, and will, cut across our self-life in terms of our opinions, our ideas, our cherished traditions, and such other facets of our self-life. It must be stated again that each time there is a further revelation of Jesus Christ, it must cut across anything that is not of God. And when that happens, the Holy Spirit will apply the cross upon our lives. Are we willing to take up the cross and follow the Lord? If we are not willing, then even if we receive the light of revelation, eventually that light will fade away. Or perhaps you may still retain the knowledge but the life is gone. Hence, we see that revelation and the cross cannot be separated. Whenever you have a revelation of the Lord Jesus, you are lifted up, as it were, to the third heaven. Who, then, does not want revelation? It is so glorious. But always bear in mind that if you have such revelation, it will and must be accompanied by a thorn in your flesh; otherwise, you will be proud (cf. II Corinthians 12:1-10, esp. v.7). There must be the Spirit's dealing in us by means of the cross. These two spiritual exercises—revelation and the application of the cross—go together.

I deeply sense that it is not merely church history about which we today are considering together, but that it is also something very living and vital for us to experience in our Christian walk. How we need to be filled with the full knowledge of God's will in all wisdom and spiritual understanding.

What was the Ending of the Colossian Church?

Results of Paul's Letter and Prayer

After Paul wrote that letter to the Colossian church brethren and sent it by the hand of Tychicus, what happened when it arrived in Colossae, I have often wondered. This is a wonderful letter. And oh, how I thank God for this letter. Colossae was a small town with a little church—so tiny in size that no mention of either town or church is found in the book of

Acts; and yet, what a tremendous and extremely important letter was sent there. This shows the love of God, does it not?

Tychicus was a fellow bondman of Jesus Christ and a faithful minister (4:7a). The apostle told them in the letter that Tychicus would not only report to them what had happened to Paul himself, but he would also encourage them (4:7b-8). Thus, with Tychicus there to help them and also the presence once again of Onesimus with them as a living example of what God could do (4:9a), I have wondered what happened. Epaphras could not return to Colossae because he was now a fellow prisoner with Paul (see again Philemon 23). The apostle had said in his letter that he labored for them by prayer to the end that they might be perfected in Christ Jesus (1:9-10a, 28b, 29a). Paul as it were was laboring in combat (2:1); for when it comes to spiritual issues combat is required, since there is a spiritual battle taking place. The Enemy attempts to lead us away from Christ or else to still keep us away from Christ. That is always the Enemy's purpose. He will employ all kinds of tricks to accomplish this.

Here, though, were Paul and Epaphras who together labored and prayed, combating the Enemy in prayer on behalf of the Colossian believers (4:12-13). I therefore have wondered that with all these prayers and with such a letter having been sent, whether the Colossian believers were eventually awakened. I hope they were and that they were restored to Christ.

Similarities between the Letters to Colossae and Laodicea

After all this Colossae is no longer mentioned in the New Testament. Some thirty years later, in 95 or 96 A.D., the apostle John, on the island of Patmos, received a commission from the risen Lord to write a letter in His name to the church in Laodicea (Revelation 3:14-22). Let us recall that Colossae, Hierapolis, and Laodicea together formed a tri-city area, thus meaning that what happened to one happened to the others because they could not be separated. This is somewhat confirmed in the Letter to the Colossians wherein Paul wrote: "After you read this letter let the church in Laodicea read it, and you in turn read the letter from Laodicea" (see Colossians 4:13, 16). From this we can infer that Laodicea, Hierapolis, and Colossae were one. All three, as it were, were inseparable. So by the time of the apostle John on Patmos, Colossae was not mentioned in the book of Revelation; but Laodicea was mentioned there and hence, we can fairly accurately conclude that what happened in the Laodicean church most likely also happened in the church at Colossae. In fact, in reading the Letter to the Colossians and the letter mentioned in Revelation chapter 3 that was sent to the church in Laodicea, we find that there are certain similarities. Let us consider several of these similarities.

Revelation of Christ

In the Letter to the Colossians the Lord Jesus was revealed to them as the firstborn of all creation, signifying that all creation was created in Him, by Him, and for Him (1:15b-16). We are also told in that letter that He is the Head of the church which is His body. He thus has the first place in all things (1:18).

In the letter sent to the church in Laodicea, how did the risen Lord reveal himself to them? He said this: "I am the Amen, the true and faithful witness, the beginning of the creation of God" (see Revelation 3:14). Here we discern certain similarities in the revelation presented to the Colossian believers and to the church in Laodicea.

Condition

When we look into the spiritual state of these two churches as is revealed in these two letters, we learn that the condition of the Colossian believers, as we saw earlier, was that instead of staying in Christ they were being led away from Him; that instead of following Christ, they were following the world and its teaching. And as for the church in Laodicea, we learn that the believers there were neither hot nor cold but had become lukewarm (3:15-16a). Hence, another similarity can be detected.

Judgment

How did the lord judge these two groups of believers? To those saints in Colossae the Lord through Paul said this: "You are observing certain rules: do not touch, do not handle, do not taste, and so forth. Such are only adopted to boost your flesh. Such legalism does not really deal with your flesh. Yet you think that now you are spiritual, but actually your flesh is being expanded. You are deceived" (see 2:20-23). That was the Lord's judgment upon the Colossian church. And to the church in Laodicea the Lord through John judged the believers there as follows: "You think you are rich, that you lack nothing; but you are wretched, poor, naked, and blind" (3:17). How similar in judgment.

Calling

What was the calling issued to these two churches? In the letter to the Colossians, of course, the clear calling was for them to simply "Return to Christ" (cf. 2:6-8a). And in the letter to the church in Laodicea, it was: "Repent" (3:19b).

So we see that there were a number of similarities between these two letters.

Two Possibilities of How Colossae Ended

One possibility of the ending of the Colossian church is that after they received Paul's letter they returned to Christ and, by the grace of God, they truly walked in the Lord, being rooted and built up in Him (2:6-7a). They had the revelation and they had the spiritual understanding. However, after thirty years another generation arose, and that generation received the revelation as knowledge but without the necessary divine light in them. Because of this, their situation is not dissimilar from that described regarding the church in Laodicea. The latter thought they were rich in that they thought they knew everything; but actually, they were poor, blind, and naked (3:17).

Let us pause and consider that there is something we need to be warned about here. Oftentimes the first generation does have revelation and, with it, life; but when the second generation arises, they have the knowledge but no life. Now that is one possibility of what may have happened with the Colossian church.

The other possibility is that though they received such a letter and much prayer and love had been poured out upon them, they did not repent and return to Christ, and the result was that the Lord, as He had declared in His letter to Laodicea, said, "If you do not repent, I will spew you out of My mouth." It is that serious a matter.

We do very much need to take this matter to heart. Just because there is a good beginning is no warrant for us to sit back and say, "A good beginning means that our arrival at spiritual maturity in Christ is already half achieved." A good beginning does not guarantee a good end. We need to be in fear and trembling before the Lord, and the *only* protection we have is to be filled with the full knowledge of God's will in all wisdom and spiritual understanding. That is the only safeguard we can have. How we need to be before God about this. May the Lord help us.

Lord, we do believe that Thou hast a living, present message for us today through Thy written word. Lord, we pray that we may have the ears to hear. Keep us in humility, in fear and in trembling lest we be led astray. Lord, we pray that Thou wilt keep us to Thyself that we may truly walk in Thee, rooted and built up in Thee. We ask in Thy precious name. Amen.

Chapter Eleven

THE CHURCH IN ROME

Acts 28:11-15—And after three months we sailed in a ship which had wintered in the island, an Alexandrian, with the Dioscuri for its ensign. And having come to Syracuse we remained three days. Whence, going in a circuitous course, we arrived at Rhegium; and after one day, the wind having changed to south, on the second day we came to Puteoli, where, having found brethren, we were begged to stay with them seven days. And thus we went to Rome. And thence the brethren, having heard about us, came to meet us as far as Appii Forum and Tres Tabernae, whom when Paul saw, he thanked God and took courage.

Acts 28:30-31—And he remained two whole years in his own hired lodging, and received all who came to him, preaching the kingdom of God, and teaching the things concerning the Lord Jesus Christ, with all freedom unhinderedly.

Romans 1:7-12—To all that are in Rome, beloved of God, called saints: Grace to you and peace from God our Father and our Lord Jesus Christ. First, I thank my God through Jesus Christ for you all, that your faith is proclaimed in the whole world. For God is my witness, whom I serve in my spirit in the glad tidings of his Son, how unceasingly I make mention of you, always beseeching at my prayers, if any way now at least I may be prospered by the will of God to come to you. For I greatly desire to see you, that I may impart to you some spiritual gift to establish you; that is, to have mutual comfort among you, each by the faith which is in the other, both yours and mine.

Romans 16:19-20—For your obedience has reached to all. I rejoice therefore as it regards you; but I wish you to be wise as to that which is good, and simple as to evil. But the God of peace shall bruise Satan under your feet shortly. The grace of our Lord Jesus Christ be with you.

What has been shared on the life of the body of Christ, the church, will not be complete if there not be also a sharing on the life of the church in Rome. We will recall the command of Jesus that His disciples should be His witnesses from Jerusalem to all Judea and Samaria and to the end of the earth (Acts 1:8b). The church on earth began in Jerusalem and then it spread to Judea and Samaria, and upon reading the last chapter of the book of Acts we learn that it had spread to Rome as well.

Now it is quite true that we do not know too much about the life of the church in Rome; nevertheless, we gain a glimpse into its life from not only the book of Acts but also from Paul's Letter to the Romans and his Letter to the Philippians. Through these three sources we can derive a considerable amount of information regarding the life of the church in Rome and thereby learn some lessons.

The Healthy Beginning of the Church in Rome

First of all, I would like for us to see how the church in Rome began. When Paul wrote his Letter to the Romans in roughly 58 A.D., he had sent it from Corinth on the way of making his last visit to Jerusalem. Because he sensed the Lord was exercising his heart to at last visit Rome, he wrote that letter to the saints in Rome. It is quite clear that when Paul wrote the letter, the church in Rome was already in existence. As a matter of fact, from Romans 15 we learn that at the time he wrote the letter he had already been exercised for "these many years" about wanting to visit Rome (vv.23-24). So this evidences the fact that the church in Rome had experienced its beginning fairly early on.

Early Believers from Pentecost

How, though, had it begun? For this to be determined we must return to the day of Pentecost in Jerusalem when the Holy Spirit came and the 120 believers assembled in the Upper Room were baptized into one body and began to speak of the great things of God in many different languages (Acts 2:6b, 11b). On that occasion there were many people who had gathered in Jerusalem from all over the known world of that day because it was the time of the Feast of Pentecost. Acts 2 records the fact that people from many different parts of the world were in the city at that time, and that among them were visitors from Rome—both Jews and Gentile converts to Judaism (2:10b). Most likely, therefore, on that day of Pentecost a considerable number of those visitors from Rome had received the gospel. Having thus believed in the Lord Jesus, some of them very likely found their way back to Rome taking the gospel of Jesus Christ with them.

Priscilla and Aquila

We will recall how in his Romans letter Paul, in extending his greetings to the saints in Rome, had mentioned Prisca (Priscilla) and Aquila (16:3-4). We are very familiar with this couple because we found them being cited again and again in the book of Acts. They were Jews who had at various times lived in Rome. When Emperor Claudius (probably in 49 A.D.) had expelled all the Jews from Rome, this couple had gone to Corinth, where Paul in his first encounter with them had joined himself to them in their home. Not only were they a brother and sister in the Lord, they also were engaged in the same trade as Paul—tent-making. So Paul stayed with them and worked with them in their mutual trade. Most likely Aquila and Priscilla had been among those who were saved in Jerusalem on the day of Pentecost, and if so, they were among the earliest Christians to have believed the gospel. While in Corinth God used them considerably. Later on they were in Ephesus and again God used them to begin the church there. And by the time Paul wrote the Letter to the Romans, they had returned to Rome, and we again hear of the church meeting in their house (16:5a). Hence, this couple was greatly used by God; for whenever and wherever they were to be found, the church was being built up. And currently they were in Rome.

Various Types of People

In writing his Letter to the Romans Paul said, "To all who are in Rome, beloved of God, called saints" (1:7a). From this salutation alone we can conclude that there was already a group of believers in Rome; and we can also conclude from his letter that among these believers there were Jews and there were also many who were Gentiles. How do we know this? In the letter's chapter 16 are numerous greetings from Paul extended to many people whom he knew before. And it is very interesting to read the list of these greetings because there are Latin names, Greek names, and Jewish names. Thus we can see that all types of people were in the church at Rome.

For instance, we know that Aquila and Priscilla were Hellenistic Jews who had settled in Rome. Paul next said in verse 5b: "Salute Epaenetus, my beloved, who is the first-fruits of Asia for Christ." He was a Greek and he was the first convert of Paul's in the Roman province of Asia, probably at Ephesus, and he too had by this time moved to Rome. Again: "Salute Maria, who labored much for you" (v.6). Maria was a Jewish name. "Salute Andronicus and Junias, my kinsmen and fellow-captives, who were of note among the apostles; who were also in Christ before me" (v.7). These two were Jews and they had believed in the Lord before Paul. Some Bible scholars believe that probably they were also among those saved on the day of Pentecost, and that they were noteworthy among the apostles. These two had also moved to Rome.

Jews and Gentiles

In reading further into chapter 16 we continue to find additional names of Jews, of Greeks, and of names of people from Asia and other parts of the world. Rome at that time was the capital of the world, and as the saying goes, all roads led to Rome. Therefore, probably some of those people who were saved during the first days of the church in Jerusalem were now in Rome; and later those from Asia, from Greece, and from the various places where Paul had visited had also eventually found their way to Rome. And thus was the church in Rome begun; and as can be seen in the Letter to the Romans, it was composed of both Jews and Gentiles.

In his Letter to the Romans Paul sometimes addressed the Jews, and sometimes he addressed the Gentiles. For instance, in chapter 1 he addressed the Gentiles, but in chapter 2 he addressed the Jews. And in chapters 9-11 he addressed both the Jews and the Gentiles. It therefore shows that the church in Rome was composed of both Jews and Gentiles. Some observers have thought that there were more Jews than Gentiles; others claim that there were more Gentiles than Jews. We do not know for certain which was true; but what we do know for certain is this: that the church in Rome began with both Jewish and Gentile Christians.

Paul's Relationship with Brethren at Rome

Obviously many of the people in the church at Rome had had some relationship with the apostle Paul even though when he wrote the Letter to the Romans he had never been there. He had been thinking of going there since he knew a number of key people in the church at Rome. They had had some kind of previous relationship with him—as in the case of Aquila and Priscilla, who we know had had a long relationship with the apostle Paul. So even though the apostle had never visited with many of these Roman believers, there was some connection between him and the church in Rome.

Peter: the Founder of the Church in Rome?

Now according to the tradition of the Roman Catholic Church, the church in Rome had been established by Peter. As claimed in this tradition, Peter went to Rome in the second year of the reign of Emperor Claudius, 42 A.D., in order to overthrow the sorcerer magician Simon Magus mentioned in the book of Acts (8:9-24); and the apostle then stayed on in Rome for twenty-five years, becoming the first bishop of the church in Rome. All that is according to the Catholic tradition, but we know this is impossible to have occurred, for the following reasons.

First of all, Peter was with the famous council meeting in Jerusalem (see Acts 15) that had taken place in 49 or 50 A.D.; after which he had also visited Syrian Antioch (Galatians 2:11ff.). Hence, it is impossible that Peter would have been in Rome as early as 42 A.D. Second, when Paul wrote the Letter to the Romans in 58 A.D., had Peter been there, Paul would certainly have mentioned him; but he did not mention Peter in any way. Third, Paul wrote in his Romans letter (15:20) that he would not attempt laboring upon the foundation of other servants of God. Had the church in Rome been founded by Peter, then Paul would have been doing something contradictory to his own rule. But the church brethren in Rome had such a relationship with Paul that he could write to them and could go there and help them to be built up, and in so doing would not violate his own publicized principle.

It can therefore be stated clearly that Peter was not the founder of the church in Rome. Most likely Peter's presence in Rome came very late, perhaps in the latter part of 63 A.D., and he was there for only a few months prior to his being martyred in 64 A.D. So we know for certain that Peter was not the founder of the church in Rome.

Different People But a Common Faith

The church in Rome was composed not only of Jews and Gentiles but also of slaves and freemen—this according to the names we find in Romans chapter 16. Moreover, there were some saints there who belonged to noble families and some who were of the lower class. Most likely, when the gospel spread to Rome, it began with the lower class, perhaps among the slaves, and then it began to reach the higher class, that of the nobility. For let us be reminded that at the time Paul wrote from Rome his prison letter to the Philippians, he had even sent greetings from those of the household of Caesar (4:22). So the gospel had even reached into the imperial court. Thus there was a mixture of Jews and Gentiles, a mixture of different races, and of those having a different social status. Although it was a mixture of different backgrounds, even so, these brethren were together as one. Paul declared in his epistle to the Romans (see 1:8b): "Your faith is being reported all over the world."

From the human standpoint it could be said that the church at Rome was a group of believers from many different backgrounds, and yet they had a common faith; and their faith was so strong that word of it had spread to all the known world. That was nothing to be surprised at since Rome at that time was the center of that world, and from there, the news could spread with relative ease everywhere.

Obedience of Faith

In Romans 16 the apostle of Christ could write this concerning these brethren at Rome: "Your obedience has come to the knowledge of all" (v.19a mgn). Not only did they have faith, they also had the *obedience* of faith. Faith is not only a believing on someone or in something; faith is also that which is to be obeyed. So these Roman believers had not only faith in the Lord Jesus, but on the basis of their faith they also obeyed it. Or to phrase it another way, they walked according to what they believed. No wonder the condition in the church at Rome was quite healthy.

That does not mean it was a perfect church, for a serious reading of the Letter to the Romans reveals a number of hints here and there to the contrary. Why, for instance, was it felt necessary by the apostle that he should write these Roman believers such a complete treatise on the gospel of Jesus Christ—such a systematic, full and complete work on salvation? Paul evidently sensed that though they knew the gospel, they did not know the fullness of the mystery of the gospel. He wanted to share with them more concerning the gospel of Jesus Christ.

Furthermore, this letter uncovers the fact that there were some problems among these saints—for example, the receiving of one another (see chapters 14 and 15, esp. 14:1, 3; 15:7). The strong in faith were apparently looking down on the weak in faith (14:1ff.) and accordingly would not receive them because they were too weak: they were not acting on the basis of love but on that of knowledge (14:15a); and the apostle believed that needed to be corrected. Additionally, at very near the end of his letter, Paul also mentioned that there were those who were causing division, and such ones needed to be watched and from whom to be separated (16:17-18). Evidently there were some people there who wanted to bring in some teaching that would divide God's people. So the church in Rome was not a perfect one; but on the whole, it was a very healthy church.

Fervent in Love

Besides an obedient faith there was another proof of the Roman church's overall healthy state. In Paul's journey by land and sea to Rome from Asia (see Acts 27:1-28:16a) there was a shipwreck. As a result, Paul and all with him were forced to stay in Melita (Malta) for a few months until they could get into another boat that brought them finally to land on the Italian peninsula. When Paul and his party came to Puteoli, they found some brethren there and stayed with them for seven days (Acts 28:13b-14). The news of his arrival probably was carried from Puteoli to Rome; and when the brethren in Rome heard that Paul was coming and coming as a prisoner, how did they react? Did they keep themselves away from Paul lest they be found to be guilty by association? No; instead, the brethren in Rome went out to meet Paul; but bear in mind that they had to go a great distance because the Apius Forum (or Market of Appius) was forty-three miles from Rome, and Tres Tabernae (that is, Three Tabernacles or Taverns), was thirty-three miles from Rome.

So those Roman brethren went some thirty to forty miles to meet Paul (Acts 28:15a-b). Now in those days travel was quite a different matter from today with us. We can simply jump into a car and drive thirty or forty miles very quickly. But back then they had to walk the entire distance, which took some time; but what love it showed. There was a zealousness in these brethren from Rome—a fervency of brotherly love. That demonstrates again, does it not, the healthy condition of the Roman church. When Paul saw these people, he was greatly encouraged and thanked God for what these brethren did (Acts 28:15c).

Christ Was Preached

Of course, the arrival of Paul into Rome was quite an event. After he arrived, he was allowed to stay in his own hired apartment, but always with a Roman soldier guarding him (Acts 28:16, 30a). Shortly after his arrival Paul called the Jewish leaders together, and after some discussion he found some who believed and some who did not (Acts 28:17-24). Paul stayed in his rented quarters for two years (Acts 28:30a), waiting to be judged by Nero, the Emperor. During that period, Paul preached the gospel of the kingdom of God (Acts 28:31a). He also taught of the Lord Jesus Christ unhinderedly (Acts 28:31b). He had all the freedom to do that in his rented place. He received everyone who came and faithfully preached the gospel. Because of what he did, it encouraged the brothers and sisters in Rome to preach the gospel fearlessly (Philippians 1:14). Paul was a man full of fire, and that fire began to ignite a fire in the hearts of the brothers and sisters there. But there were some who preached the gospel out of contention; and most likely, they were the Judaizers who had continued to follow Paul all the way, preaching the law so as to increase the suffering of Paul. But this apostle of Christ reacted by saying: "It does not matter as long as Christ is preached" (1:15-18). Thank God for that.

Paul having come into their midst, the Praetorian guards (members of the bodyguard of the Roman Emperor) who, one after another, were chained with Paul, could not avoid overhearing Paul's gospel message. Through Paul's faithfulness a number of these palace guards within the Preatorium got saved (1:12-13); and as was noted earlier, in the household of Caesar itself a number came to the Lord. So the spiritual state of the church in Rome was quite healthy and good along several lines of observation. Let us consider each of these more closely.

The Life of the Church in Rome

If we look into the life of the church in Rome, there are several aspects which I believe will truly touch our hearts. One is what we have briefly touched upon earlier, and it centers around the fact that the church in Rome was composed of so many different people.

No Distinctions in Christ

There were all kinds of distinctions, especially in the matter of race. Generally speaking, it could be said that in Roman society the Jews and the Gentiles constituted a big problem because the Jews would have nothing to do with the Gentiles. The Jews considered themselves as the chosen people of God and thus they looked down upon the Gentiles as unclean, as dogs. They would not even enter the house of a Gentile, much less eat with them. Of course, there was a reaction on the part of the Gentiles towards them, so that the Gentiles despised the Jews. They looked down upon them and considered them as nothing. There was no social relationship between these two groups at that time. But when the gospel made its appearance, the wall of partition between the Jews and Gentiles was broken down through the cross (Ephesians 2:11-18 ASV). On the cross of the Lord Jesus, God took away this huge distinction—insurmountable, humanly speaking. That enmity was removed and He brought these two groups of people together as brothers and sisters. This is marvelous. Such is the power of the gospel.

In Christ the Jews and the Gentiles are made one, and to such an extent that in Christ and in the church there is neither Jew nor Gentile. When a Jew comes to Christ, the Jew is gone. When a Gentile comes to Christ, the Gentile too is gone. In Christ we have only Him—no Jew, no Gentile. And likewise in the church there is no Jew, no Gentile, only Christ in you, in me, in all of us. Now that is the marvel of the gospel, and it happened in Rome—especially in Rome.

Also in the church at Rome there were both slaves and freemen. This was another huge challenge during that time because in the Roman Empire there were more slaves than freemen. Only the Romans were free persons who enjoyed their particular rights as citizens of the Empire. The slaves had no rights of any kind. Yet in the church at Rome the slaves and the freemen sat together in the assembly of the brethren in Christ. That distinction was gone in the church. Rome was the capital city and that was where the freemen and their freedom began, yet both the slaves and the freemen were together as one in the church.

Then there was a further social distinction—this one between the lower class and the upper class. It was a real problem back then in Roman society. Recently, a brother went on a visit to Chile in South America, and when he came back he reported to us that in Chile the distinction between the rich and the poor is so great that the two have nothing to do with each other. Yet by this time the Lord was able to bring the rich and the poor together in the church in Chile, and it was a beautiful thing to behold. So in the church, there is neither Jew nor Gentile, neither barbarian nor Scythian, neither the circumcised nor uncircumcised, neither bondman nor freeman; neither rich nor poor; instead, it is Christ who is all and in all (see Colossians 3:11). What a wonderful thing this was in the church at Rome.

Let me reiterate that the brethren were not perfect in the Roman church because they still had some problems in the matter of receiving one another, but the Lord dealt with that. How we thank God that He can put us together in Christ in the church as one. In the world you may be an American, a Chinese, an Irishman, a Norwegian; but in the church we have no American, we have no Chinese, we have no Irishman, we have no Norwegian. We only have Christ. We do not see an

American here; we see Christ. We do not see a Chinese here; we see Christ. We do not see an Irishman here; we see Christ. We do not see a Norwegian here; we see Christ. Let us constantly remember that. Are we totally delivered? We need to be totally delivered from all these distinctions, because in Christ in the church there is but one—Christ and Christ only. He is all and in all, and this we can see very clearly in the church at Rome.

The Labor of the Sisters

Among the many greetings of Paul in Romans chapter 16 he mentioned a number of people who were in the Roman church. There were men and there were women. I wonder, have you ever counted how many women Paul mentioned there in that concluding chapter of his Letter to the Romans? It is perhaps not easy because we cannot be sure due to the foreign nature of some of the names shown there; nevertheless, I believe there are at least seven or eight names which are those of women.

Prisca was a woman, and interestingly, her name is placed before that of Aquila because it seems as though she was more involved in the work of God than her husband, even though her husband was with her and the meeting of the church was in their home. Aquila, being the head of the household, had to be responsible, but so far as the work was concerned, Prisca was more involved than Aquila. She probably knew the Lord more than her husband, and because of that she probably was the one who had helped Apollos at Ephesus in understanding the way of God more exactly (Acts 18:24-26). Nevertheless, they both were Paul's fellow workers, risking their necks for Paul (Romans 16:3-4a). We do not find that fact cited in the book of Acts. In that book we find that Paul was in prison four times, but some people have claimed that Paul actually was in prison seven times. When and where the other three times were, we do not know. I do not know when Aquila and Priscilla risked their necks for Paul, but they truly loved him and risked their lives for him. Moreover, all the Gentile churches owed something to this couple, as the apostle made clear in Romans 16 (v.4b).

Then there was Maria, a sister in the church at Rome, who labored much in the Lord. There were two girls, Tryphaena and Tryphosa, who labored in the Lord. Then there was Persis, the beloved, who labored much in the Lord. The name Persis is probably a Persian one; most likely, therefore, she was a sister from Persia who labored much in the Lord.

The mentioning of a number of sisters as well as brothers indicates that in the Roman church both the men and the women functioned together. As members of the body of Christ they all functioned according to the gift and the grace that God had given to each (Romans 12:6a), and they were faithful in their work.

It is very touching to find that Paul mentioned especially how the sisters labored much in the Lord. Whenever you go to this or that assembly of believers, you will probably find that the sisters are usually laboring more than the brothers. The brothers may receive the credit, but the sisters are actually doing the work. Paul noticed that and God noticed it. So be encouraged, you sisters; labor much in the Lord. The whole church in Rome—all the members of the body of Christ there— seemed to work together; each was faithful in what the Lord had given. No wonder the church in Rome was healthy. That is something for us to learn, too.

The Assembling Together

Among the many greetings of Paul he wrote this: "Greet Prisca and Aquila ... and the assembly [or, church] at their house" (16:3a, 5a). The church at that time met in their house. It was probably not until after the first century that there were buildings used especially for the gathering of the saints. But in the early days they usually met in homes, and Aquila and Priscilla had opened their home for the Roman saints to meet in. Yet, among these same greetings of Paul there were not only individuals who were greeted but also groups. There he wrote as follows: "Salute those who belong to Narcissus, who are in the Lord. Salute Asyncritus, Phlegon, Hermes, Patrobas, Hermas, and the brethren with them. Salute Philologus, and Julia, Nereus, and his sister, and Olympas, and all the saints with them" (16:11b, 14-15). These were different groups of believers in Rome.

Because Rome was a big city and there were many brothers and sisters there, they most likely lived in different sections of the city. Some may have lived in the Jewish sections, some may have lived in the Gentile sections, and so forth. Perhaps during the weekdays they just met in groups, but they would come together as the entire church on the Lord's day to meet in the house of Aquila and Priscilla. That is another thing we can learn from the life of the church in Rome. When there are more people and they are widely spread out, then probably there can be small groups meeting during the weekdays, but on the Lord's day they can all come and meet together as a church. That is what we find in the church at Rome.

The Endurance of the Church in Rome

Most likely Paul was in Rome for two years during his first imprisonment, waiting to be judged. In the early part of his reign, Nero was not that wicked and evil; so he evidently allowed the gospel to be preached openly without any hindrance. He had Paul acquitted and thus the apostle was able to travel again. Paul revisited some places and probably he went to Spain, as he had desired to do (Romans 15:24a, 28). Perhaps during that period after Paul was released and was away, Peter came to Rome, most likely in the latter part of 63 A.D.

Now We See the Church

It was in 64 A.D., however, that Nero set Rome on fire. After he burned the city of Rome, Nero searched for a scapegoat on whom to pin responsibility for the crime; and the Christians became an easy target to accuse, since they were different from the world. So the wicked Emperor accused the Christians of having set Rome ablaze, and great persecution ensued. Even Roman historians acknowledge that these Christians were persecuted out of jealousy and envy. It was not because they did anything wrong; it was not because of any arson having been perpetrated by them. It was simply because they were a ready target for Nero to accuse. Many Christians were seized. Some were sewn in the skins of beasts and thrown to the wild dogs to be torn asunder; some were tied to trees with oil poured on them and then set ablaze as lanterns at night. Many, many suffered martyrdom for the Lord's sake.

Paul was rearrested, and thus both Peter and Paul died in Rome. Because Peter was a Jew, he was crucified; and legend says that when Peter was crucified, he said, "I am not worthy to be crucified like my Lord; crucify me upside down." Because Paul—though a Jew—was a Roman citizen, he was beheaded.

Many, many Christians died for their faith. As has been said, "The blood of the martyrs is the seed of the church." Now because of all these persecutions, Christians had to meet secretly in catacombs, which actually became their dwelling place. They lived in the catacombs, and because there was no air or sunlight, they grew pale and were weakened physically. When they died, they were buried in the catacombs. Yet, though the Christians were persecuted, it was not the church that was destroyed but it was Rome.

Conclusion

LESSONS TO BE LEARNED

Romans 15:4—For as many things as have been written before have been written for our instruction, that through endurance and through encouragement of the scriptures we might have hope.

I Corinthians 10:11—Now all these things happened to them as types, and have been written for our admonition, upon whom the ends of the ages are come.

In concluding this series of messages on the life of the various churches which are to be found in the narrative of Acts and what can be found in several of the apostle Paul's epistles, what lessons can we draw which we in our own day as members of the church, the body of Christ, can learn? I believe there are four key ones with which I would like to end our several considerations together over these past months.

Lesson One: Christ Is Living

The first lesson we can learn or learn more deeply is that Christ is living. It is evident that the Lord Jesus is living. Though He died, yet He lives; and He lives forevermore. We find that He is still speaking and is still working. In the book of Acts Luke had begun his discourse by saying that in his former treatise he had written about the Lord Jesus and how He had begun to speak, to teach, and to act. And that was the Gospel of Luke. His second treatise or discourse, the book of Acts, is a continuation of the speaking and the working of the same Lord.

In the Gospel according to Luke the Lord Jesus had taught and worked in that incarnated body of His. In the book of Acts, however, and since Christ is now the risen and ascended Lord and Head of the church which is His mystical corporate body, He teaches and acts today in that corporate body. It shows that He is living today on earth just as He had lived on earth two thousand years ago.

That is the reason the book of Acts has no ending. We noticed that it stopped abruptly with really no ending. Why so? It is because the book of Acts is continually being written further, even today. So when we read and delve into the life of the church, the body of Christ, one thing we learn and we know is that our Lord is still living in our day. He is as much alive today as He was two thousand years ago. He is still teaching and He is still working in and through His church.

Lesson Two: The Lord Is Building His Church

The second lesson we can learn is this: Jesus said, "I will build My church, and the gates of Hades shall not prevail against it." It is very evident in reading the book of Acts that whenever and wherever the Lord is building His church, all the gates of Hades are opened bringing forth persecution, tribulation, suffering, afflictions of every kind, temptations, and attacks; yet the gates of Hades shall not prevail against the church. It is the church triumphant. Yes, it is a suffering church, but it is a triumphant church—just as the Lord Jesus had suffered while He was on earth before He entered into His glory. So we do thank God that the Lord is building His church. No matter how His church suffers, it always ends up triumphant; and that encourages us.

We brethren must experience many tribulations if we are to enter the kingdom of God. Let us not assume that we can have smooth sailing through this world, for we are living in an alien and inhospitable world for the Christian, and the current ruler of this world, Satan, is an usurper. If we are faithful to the Lord, we will be attacked, we will be misunderstood, we will be persecuted, we will suffer; but such is that which we can expect. It is not to be viewed as something strange, even as the apostle Peter has written in his epistle. Let us not consider it as strange because after suffering, there will be glory (I Peter 4:12-13); the Lord will surely build His church.

Lesson Three: No Perfect Church on Earth

The third lesson we can learn is that there is no perfect church on this earth. Thank God, there are some churches that are more healthy than others; also, there are some churches that are very sick. But we know that in spite of all the problems and difficulties which the church must experience or endure, the grace of God is always sufficient. He is able to use these problems, troubles, difficulties and crises to bring us into that fullness of himself. If we have very smooth sailing in church life, we will not be able to learn many other precious lessons. We will not be able to come into fullness. One way to come into fullness is by being challenged. There need to be problems, troubles, the work of the Enemy, the work of the flesh—indeed, all kinds of challenges. But God allows these things to occur that we may learn the supremacy and all-sufficiency of Christ and of His grace. For by this means the bride of Christ will be made ready. That is something of which we have the assurance.

Lesson Four: Follow the Footsteps of the Flock

In going through the book of Acts we discover the footsteps of the flock. Where can we find the Lord? In type and symbol we see that the virgin in the Song of Solomon had a heart for her Shepherd-Lord; and because she sought Him so earnestly, she was misunderstood by her brothers. They thought she was lazy. So they put her to work in many activities, to such an extent that she felt her spiritual situation had greatly suffered.

She therefore cried out to her Shepherd-Lord, saying: "Lord, where are You? Why should I be wandering with Your shepherds' flocks? Where do You feed *Your* flock? I want You." And her Shepherd-Lord replied, "Follow the footsteps of the flock" (see Song 1:5-8).

I do believe that from the beginning to the end of the church age, there are manifested the footsteps of the flock. It is very strange that in this Song of Solomon the virgin cries out: "Your shepherds' flocks." It is a double plural number here—both shepherds and flocks. We find in Christianity in the world today many shepherds and many flocks: "This is my flock," says one shepherd; or "That is my flock," claims another shepherd. Such confuses us; but thank God, there is *the* flock, the Lord's only one flock.

In John 10 Jesus is recorded as saying: "I have other sheep not of this fold. I will bring them together—and there shall be one flock, one Shepherd." The Jews are a fold; the Gentiles are another fold; but that is not a flock. The Lord will bring the Jews and Gentiles out of their folds and make them one flock with one shepherd—even the Lord Jesus. We have one Shepherd and there is but one flock. That is the flock which faithfully follows the Shepherd in His footsteps wherever He goes. So their footsteps—those of the flock—are the footsteps of the Shepherd. By following their footsteps, you will find the Shepherd. And so, I believe that the book of Acts shows us the footsteps of the flock, and by noticing, observing, and following the footsteps of the faithful flock, we shall find the Shepherd. So may the Lord help us.

Dear Lord, we thank Thee for allowing us to fellowship on the life of the church, the body of Christ. Lord, we do ask Thee that what Thou dost want to teach us will not be snatched away by the Enemy; but Lord, by Thy Spirit, Thou wilt register these things in our hearts and make them reality to us, so that we may by Thy grace avoid all the pitfalls; and that we may also be built up together according to Thy will. Lord, our only desire is that Thou art able to express Thyself through Thy church today. We ask in Thy precious name. Amen.

TITLES AVAILABLE
From Christian Fellowship Publishers

By Watchman Nee

Aids to "Revelation"	The Life That Wins
Amazing Grace	The Lord My Portion
Back to the Cross	The Messenger of the Cross
A Balanced Christian Life	The Ministry of God's Word
The Better Covenant	My Spiritual Journey
The Body of Christ: A Reality	The Mystery of Creation
The Character of God's Workman	Powerful According to God
Christ the Sum of All Spiritual Things	Practical Issues of This Life
The Church and the Work – 3 Vols	The Prayer Ministry of the Church
The Church in the Eternal Purpose of God	The Release of the Spirit
"Come, Lord Jesus"	Revive Thy Work
The Communion of the Holy Spirit	The Salvation of the Soul
The Finest of the Wheat – Vol. 1	The Secret of Christian Living
The Finest of the Wheat – Vol. 2	Serve in Spirit
From Faith to Faith	The Spirit of Judgment
From Glory to Glory	The Spirit of the Gospel
Full of Grace and Truth – Vol. 1	The Spirit of Wisdom and Revelation
Full of Grace and Truth – Vol. 2	Spiritual Authority
Gleanings in the Fields of Boaz	Spiritual Discernment
The Glory of His Life	Spiritual Exercise
God's Plan and the Overcomers	Spiritual Knowledge
God's Work	The Spiritual Man
Gospel Dialogue	Spiritual Reality or Obsession
Grace for Grace	Take Heed
Heart-to-Heart Talks	The Testimony of God
Interpreting Matthew	Whom Shall I Send?
Journeying towards the Spiritual	The Word of the Cross
The King and the Kingdom of Heaven	Worship God
The Latent Power of the Soul	Ye Search the Scriptures
Let Us Pray	

The Basic Lesson Series
Vol. 1 - A Living Sacrifice
Vol. 2 - The Good Confession
Vol. 3 - Assembling Together
Vol. 4 - Not I, But Christ
Vol. 5 - Do All to the Glory of God
Vol. 6 - Love One Another

ORDER FROM: 11515 Allecingie Parkway Richmond, VA 23235
www.c-f-p.com

TITLES AVAILABLE
From Christian Fellowship Publishers

By Stephen Kaung

"But We See Jesus"
  —*Messages on the Life of the Lord Jesus*
Discipled to Christ
God's Purpose for the Family
The Gymnasium of Christ
In the Footsteps of Christ
New Covenant Living & Ministry
Now We See the Church
  —*Messages on the Life of the Church, the Body of Christ*
Shepherding
The Songs of Degrees
  —*Meditations on Fifteen Psalms*
The Splendor of His Ways
  —*Seeing the Lord's End in Job*

The "God Has Spoken" Series
Seeing Christ in the Old Testament, Part One
Seeing Christ in the Old Testament, Part Two
Seeing Christ in the New Testament

ORDER FROM: 11515 Allecingie Parkway Richmond, VA 23235
www.c-f-p.com